ANGER

TAMING A POWERFUL EMOTION

Gary Chapman

MOODY PUBLISHERS

CHICAGO

Unless otherwise indicated, all Scripture quotations are taken from the Holy Bible, New Living Translation, copyright © 1996, 2004, 2007 2013 by permission of Tyndale House Foundation. Used by permission of Tyndale House Publishers, Inc., Carol Stream, Illinois 60188, U.S.A. All rights reserved.

Scripture quotations marked NIV are taken from the Holy Bible, New International Version®, NIV®. Copyright © 1973, 1978, 1984, 2011 by Biblica, Inc.™ Used by permission of Zondervan. All rights reserved worldwide. www.zondervan.com. The "NIV" and "New International Version" are trademarks registered in the United States Patent and Trademark Office by Biblica, Inc.™

Edited by Elizabeth Cody Newenhuyse
Cover and interior design: Erik M. Peterson
Cover photo of flag copyright © 2007 by ROMAOSLO/iStock. All rights reserved.
Author photo: P.S. Photography

Library of Congress Cataloging-in-Publication Data
Chapman, Gary D.,
    [Other side of love]
    Anger : taming a powerful emotion / Gary D Chapman.
        pages cm
    Summary: "A relative makes a tactless comment about your child's weight. The guy behind you on the expressway follows too closely. Your spouse lets the gas tank go down to empty . . . again. Getting angry is easy. Daily irritations, frustrations, and pain poke at us. Feelings of disappointment, hurt, rejection, and embarrassment prod in us. And once the unwieldy cluster of emotions of anger are aroused, our thoughts and actions can feel out of control and impossible to manage." Dr. Gary Chapman, #1 New York Times bestselling author of The 5 Love Languages
    Rev. ed. of: The other side of love, © 1999.
    Includes bibliographical references.
    ISBN 978-0-8024-1314-7 (paperback)
    1. Anger—Religious aspects—Christianity. I. Title.
    BV4627.A5C48 2015
    241'.3—dc23
                        2015003647

We hope you enjoy this book from Moody Publishers. Our goal is to provide high-quality, thought-provoking books and products that connect truth to your real needs and challenges. For more information on other books and products written and produced from a biblical perspective, go to www.moodypublishers.com or write to:

Moody Publishers
820 N. LaSalle Boulevard
Chicago, IL 60610

5 7 9 10 8 6

Printed in the United States of America

*To those individuals who over the years have
shared with me their personal struggles with anger
and in so doing forced me to search for answers
to the troublesome experience of anger*

CONTENTS

QUICK TAKES

For a brief overview of each chapter, turn to these "Quick Takes."

OUR ANGRY WORLD

Anger is everywhere. Spouses are angry at each other. Employees are angry at bosses. Teens are angry at parents (and vice versa). Citizens are angry at their government. Television news routinely shows angry demonstrators shouting their wrath or the weeping mother of a teen gunned down in an angry quarrel. Spend some time around a major airport when bad weather has canceled flights, and you will observe anger in action.

Many of us are angry at ourselves. Sometimes we are angry and think we "shouldn't feel that way." Or we observe our children expressing anger inappropriately and wonder how to teach them to deal with their anger.

Clearly, many of us have issues with anger. In addition, Christians are often confused about this powerful and complex emotion. For those who follow Christ, is there ever an appropriate expression of anger? What does the Bible say? Can anger ever be a *good* thing?

If, in searching for answers to these questions, you go online and type "anger" into a search engine, you will find an overwhelming amount of information. Yet most of what has been written does not deal with two fundamental questions: What is the *origin* of anger, and what is the *purpose* of anger? Why do men and women experience the emotion of anger? Understanding the origin of anger is essential to understanding the purpose of anger, and understanding the purpose of anger is essential to learning how to process anger in a constructive manner.

The few books and articles that do raise the question of origins tend to see anger as a survival technique in humans' early evolutionary development. Anger is "nature's way" of preparing humans to respond in times of danger. As one who holds undergraduate and graduate degrees in the field of anthropology, I believe this view is woefully inadequate. In the first place, it ignores the Christian worldview; and secondly, even if one accepts a naturalistic worldview, it does not adequately explain the psychological aspects of anger.

Much of the confusion among Christians about the emotion of anger flows from a misunderstanding of the origin of anger. Christian literature on anger has tended to focus on controlling it—without an adequate understanding of the source of anger. But I am convinced that our efforts at controlling anger will be much more effective if we have a clearer understanding of the source of anger.

So where does anger come from? What is its origin? The answer, which may surprise you, is found in chapter 1—and the answer suggests anger's purpose, which is described in chapter 2.

I have counseled couples and families for many years now. I have worked with hundreds of families dealing with multiple family problems. In almost all cases, these families or couples have struggled with processing anger. When adults know how to deal with their own anger in healthy, positive ways, they not only create a more secure environment for the family; they also have greater potential for teaching their children how to process anger. Equally important, they are able to build a productive work environment, engaging effectively with their coworkers. When adults have *not* learned to process their anger, marital and family turmoil usually results, sometimes spilling over at work or other settings.

Where do we go to learn to process anger? For many of us, the answer is the counselor's office. Unfortunately, most people do not go for counseling until their mismanagement of anger has gotten them into serious trouble. Thousands of others who are already in serious trouble never go for counseling at all.

Perhaps you cannot (because of time, money, or fear) step into the counselor's office. I believe that much of what is learned in the counseling office could be learned in the living room if adults had adequate information. This book is an attempt to put into readable form the insights and techniques that have helped hundreds of couples and single adults discover a better way to process anger. The names of all clients have been changed, but their situations and conversations are real. At times, you may recognize issues and responses similar to your own. All of us can learn much about processing our anger more effectively.

If you, or someone you love, is struggling with anger, I hope this volume will help you gain a fresh—and Christian—perspective on anger. I also hope that as you gain this new perspective, you will be equipped to understand and deal with your anger or that of someone close to you. Additionally, my hope is that this book will provide interested individuals with a tool that will stimulate group discussion and workshops on the topic of anger. The discussion guide online at www.5lovelanguages.com will help you review key ideas and apply them to your life. I am convinced that much can be learned about anger in an educational setting (a small group, a Sunday school class, or seminar) as well as in the counseling office. In fact, this must happen if we are going to turn the tide on the epidemic of verbal and physical abuse that characterizes our generation.

When we bring our anger under the lordship of Christ—when we learn from a holy God about the origin and purpose of anger—we can heal our relationships. Most important, we can accomplish God's good purposes.

—Gary Chapman

Anyone can become angry—
that is easy,
but to be angry with the
right person at the right time,
and for the right purpose
and in the right way—
that is not within everyone's
power, and that is not easy.

ARISTOTLE

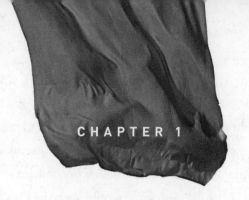

CHAPTER 1

WHERE DOES ANGER COME FROM?

Perhaps you can identify with Brooke.

Brooke, the mother of two preschoolers, loved her husband, Glen, an up-and-coming attorney. The couple had been married eight years. Brooke was a certified public accountant but had chosen to put her career on hold until the children started school.

"I think I made a mistake," she told me. "I don't think I am cut out to be a mother. I always wanted children, but now that I've got them, I don't like the way I treat them. And I don't like what they do to me. I don't ever remember being angry or losing my temper before I had children. I always considered myself to be in control of my emotions. But I have to admit, I have often lost it with my kids. I hate myself when I do that."

"What do you do when you lose it with the children?" I inquired.

"Different things," she said. "Sometimes I yell at them. Sometimes I spank them really hard. The other day I picked up Ginger and shook her. That really scared me. I had seen on television just the day before a report of a mother who actually killed her child by shaking her. I don't want to hurt my children. I love them, but I just lose control. I wish Glen would keep the kids and give me a break, but he is so stressed in his job that he says he doesn't feel like caring for them. I think maybe I should go back to work and let someone else take care of the children."

As I talked further with Brooke, I discovered that she was angry not only with her children's behavior but also with Glen for giving her so little help. She was angry at herself for choosing to be a full-time mom, and ultimately she was angry with God for allowing her to be a mother. "He should have known that I wouldn't be able to handle this," she said.

By now Brooke was crying. To be honest, I felt like crying too, as I remembered the hundreds of mothers who have passed through my office over the years, feeling guilty, feeling alone, not liking their kids or themselves very much.

Then there was Rich, who came to my office well dressed, but I noticed his right foot was shoeless. I soon found out why.

"I've got to have help," he began. "I've known for a long time that my anger was getting out of control, but Saturday was the last straw. For fifteen minutes, I tried to get my lawnmower started. I checked the gas, I checked the oil, I put in a new sparkplug, and still it wouldn't start. Finally, I got so exasperated that I stepped back and kicked the thing. I broke two toes and cut a third. Sitting on the steps in pain, I said to myself, 'That was really stupid.'

"I'm embarrassed. I can't tell people what really happened, so

I've been saying, 'I had an accident with a lawnmower.'

"This is not the first time I've lost my temper," he continued. "I've said some pretty nasty things to my wife and children in the past. I don't think I have ever physically abused them, but I've come close."

In the course of our conversation I discovered that Rich was highly educated, holding an MBA degree. He was married with two children, profitably employed, and owned a nice house in suburbia. Rich was an active member of his church and well respected in the community. Yet he had a habit of "blowing his cool."

Thousands of men can readily identify with Rich. Unfortunately, many of them are not as honest as he, and even fewer of them are willing to reach out for help.

Rich, with his broken toes, and Brooke, with her broken heart, are dealing with very different challenges. However, what they hold in common is the human experience of intense anger and their inability to handle it. Both knew that their anger had led them to inappropriate behavior, but neither knew what to do about it. Thus, they suffered physically and emotionally from their destructive responses to anger—and their loved ones were suffering too.

> **ANGER IS THE OPPOSITE OF THE FEELING OF LOVE. LOVE DRAWS YOU TOWARD THE PERSON; ANGER SETS YOU AGAINST THE PERSON.**

WHAT HAPPENS WHEN WE GET ANGRY?

People of all ages and social status experience anger. Brian, a high school student, is angry at the teacher who gave him a D on his report card. Liz, Brian's teacher, is angry with her ex for failing to send the child-support checks on time. Maria, an eighty-five-year-old grandmother, is angry with her oldest son, who seldom comes to see her; her son, Alex, is angry in general because he can't find a job and feels rejected by society. Marvin, a pastor, is angry with church leadership who always shoot down his best ideas. Bethany is only three years old, but she is angry with her mother, who took away her favorite toy.

But what do we mean by anger? The dictionary describes *anger* as "a strong passion or emotion of displeasure, and usually antagonism, excited by a sense of injury or insult."[1] Although we normally think of anger as an emotion, it is in reality a cluster of emotions involving the body, the mind, and the will.

And we don't sit down and say, "I think I will now experience anger." Anger is a *response* to some event or situation in life that causes us irritation, frustration, pain, or other displeasure. Thousands of events and situations have the potential for provoking anger. An elderly relative makes a tactless comment about your child's weight. The guy behind you on the expressway follows too closely. A friend is always posting political rants on Facebook. Your father was always angry about something when you were growing up, and now you have trouble managing your own anger.

Anger is fed by feelings of disappointment, hurt, rejection, and embarrassment. Anger pits you against the person, place, or thing that sparked the emotion. It is the opposite of the feeling of love. Love draws you toward the person; anger sets you against the person.

But the mind is also active from the very beginning. For example, if Becky asks her husband, Tim, to mow the lawn while she takes the kids shopping, and she comes home hours later and the grass is still shaggy, she may think, *If he cared, he would mow the lawn. He knows how much it means to me. I don't ask for much. What was he doing instead? What HE wanted to do. How selfish.* But Tim responds inwardly, *Look at everything else I've been doing! I sealed the deck, took out the garbage, and walked the dog. What does she want?*

Meanwhile, Ken sits simmering in his department's conference room while Corey, his manager, tells him his numbers are down this quarter; and if he doesn't start producing, the company might have to let him go. *It's because I'm over fifty*, Ken thinks. *They're trying to get rid of all the old guys. Corey is what, about thirty-five? What does he know?*

Becky, Tim, and Ken are all experiencing strong negative emotions—in their minds. But there's more. The body also gets in on the experience of anger. The body's autonomic nervous system "gets the adrenaline flowing." Depending upon the level of anger, any or all of the following may happen physically. The adrenal glands release two hormones: epinephrine (adrenaline) and norepinephrine (noradrenaline). These two chemicals seem to give people the arousal, the tenseness, the excitement, the heat of anger, and in turn these hormones affect the heart rate, blood pressure, lung function, and digestive tract activity.[2] So as Ken sits in the conference room listening to his boss, he can feel his face flushing, his stomach churning, and his fists clenching. It is these physiological changes that give people the feeling of being overwhelmed by anger and being unable to control it.

Then the anger spills over into action: Brooke shakes her preschooler, Bethany throws a tantrum, Rich kicks the lawnmower, and Ken returns to his cubicle and starts to compose a furious email.

We can't control our bodily reactions; however, we *can* control our mental and physical responses to anger. We'll look at that in upcoming chapters.

WHY ANGER?

But first, let's look again at the roots of anger: where it comes from and why we experience it.

I believe that the human capacity for anger is rooted in the nature of God. Please do not think that I am being disrespectful of God. On the contrary, I stand in deep reverence of God when I suggest that human anger is rooted in the divine nature. Further, I am not suggesting that anger is an essential part of the nature of God. I am suggesting that anger derives from two aspects of God's divine nature: God's holiness and God's love.

The Scriptures proclaim that God is holy. (See, for example, 1 Peter 1:16; Leviticus 11:44–45.) The word *holy* means "set apart from sin." Whether we are talking about God the Father, God the Son, or God the Spirit, there is no sin in the nature of God. The New Testament writer said of Jesus that He "faced all of the same testings we do, yet he did not sin" (Hebrews 4:15).

A second fundamental characteristic of the nature of God is love. The apostle John summarized the whole teaching of Scripture when he said simply, "God *is* love" (1 John 4:8, italics added). Love is not to be equated with God; rather, in His essential nature God is loving. This is not simply the New Testament concept of God. From beginning to end, the Scriptures reveal God as committed to the well-being of His creatures. It is God's nature to love.

It is from these two divine characteristics that God's anger is derived. Please note: The Scriptures never say, "God is anger." That statement is not, in fact, true. Anger is not a part of the essential nature of God. However, the Bible often indicates that God *experiences* anger. The word *anger* is found 455 times in the Old Testament; 375 of these refer to God's anger. In fact, the psalmist said, "God is angry with the wicked every day" (Psalm 7:11 KJV).

God's anger was not limited to Old Testament times. Read the life of Jesus, and you will see numerous occasions where Jesus demonstrated anger. (For example, see Mark 3:1–5; John 2:13–17.) *Because* God is holy and *because* God is love, God necessarily experiences anger. His love seeks only the good of His creatures. His holiness stands forever against sin. All of God's moral laws are based upon His holiness and His love; that is, they are always aligned with what is right, and they are always for the good of His creatures.

God desires humans to do what is right and enjoy the benefits. He said to ancient Israel, "Now listen! Today I am giving you a choice between life and death, between prosperity and disaster. For I command you this day to love the LORD your God and to keep his commands, decrees, and regulations by walking in his ways. If you do this, you will live and multiply, and the LORD your God will bless you and the land you are about to enter and occupy" (Deuteronomy 30:15–16).

Knowing the detrimental effects of man's sin, God's anger is kindled. It is God's concern for justice and righteousness (both of which grow

THE SCRIPTURES NEVER SAY, "GOD IS ANGER."

out of His holiness and His love) that stir God's anger. Thus, when God sees evil, anger is His logical response to injustice or unrighteousness.

"THAT'S NOT RIGHT"

So what does all of this have to do with human anger? The Scriptures say that we are made "in the image of God" (Genesis 1:27). Though that image was marred by the fall, it was not erased. People still bear the imprint of God's image deep within their souls. Thus, even though we are fallen, we still have some concern for justice and rightness. Find the most pagan man you know and follow him for a week, and you will hear him make such statements as: "That's not right. He shouldn't do that to her. She treated him wrongly." Steal his car and see if he expresses anger. Slander his daughter or wife or girlfriend and you will find that suddenly he is an extremely moral creature, condemning your action outright.

Listen to the young child who is beginning to put words into sentences, and you will soon hear the child say, "That's not fair, Mommy." Where did the child obtain that moral judgment? I suggest that it is stamped deep within his nature, tempered by parental teaching, to be sure, but the child knows when he or she has been wronged and will express it freely.

Anger, then, is the emotion that arises whenever we encounter what we perceive to be wrong. The emotional, physiological, and cognitive dimensions of anger leap to the front burner of our experience when we encounter injustice.

Why does a wife experience anger toward her husband? Because in her mind he has disappointed, embarrassed, humiliated, or rejected her. In short, he has "done her wrong." Why do teenagers experience anger toward parents? Because the teenager perceives that the parents have been unfair, unloving, unkind—that the parents have done wrong. Why does a man kick his lawnmower? Because the lawnmower is not "working right." The machine, or its manufacturer, has done him wrong. Why do drivers honk their horns when the traffic light turns green? Because they reason that the person in front of them "*should* be paying attention to the light and not texting and should have accelerated two seconds earlier."

Try to remember the last time you experienced anger and ask the question: Why did I get angry? Chances are your answer will mention some injustice. Someone or something did not treat you fairly. Something was wrong. Your anger may have been directed toward a person, an object, a situation, yourself, or God, but in every instance someone or something treated you wrongly. We are not discussing whether your perception of wrong is valid or invalid. We will deal with that in a later chapter. What we are establishing is that anger originates in the perception that something is wrong and that this sense of morality (some things are right and some things are wrong) finds its root in the fact that we are created in the image of a God who is holy and has established moral law for the good of His creatures.

Anger is not evil; anger is not sinful; anger is not a part of our fallen nature; anger is not Satan at work in our lives. Quite the contrary. Anger is evidence that we are made in God's image; it demonstrates that we still have some concern for justice and righteousness in spite of our fallen estate. The capacity for anger is strong evidence that we are more than mere animals. It reveals our concern for rightness, justice, and fairness. The experience of anger is evidence of our nobility, not our depravity.

We should thank God for our capacity to experience anger. When one ceases to experience anger, one has lost her sense of moral concern. Without moral concern, the world would be a dreadful place indeed. That brings us to our second major question: What is the purpose of anger? More to the point, what is *God's* purpose for human anger?

A man is about as big as
the things that make him angry.

WINSTON CHURCHILL

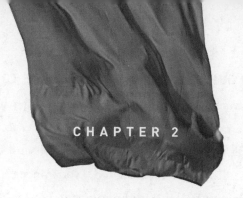

CHAPTER 2

WHEN ANGER CAN DO GOOD

When we're in the midst of an argument with our spouse or grumbling at our slow Internet, the question of God's purpose in anger might seem theoretical. Indeed, we might think human anger would displease God.

But I believe that *human anger is designed by God to motivate us to take constructive action* in the face of wrongdoing or when facing injustice.

We don't understand this very well because usually we get angry when things don't go our way—like when a page is taking forever to load when we're trying to apply for a job. We will talk further about valid and invalid anger, but our purpose here is to return to the foundational question: What is God's purpose in human anger? The answer is, anger is designed to motivate us to take positive action when we encounter injustice. I believe this is illustrated by God Himself.

FOR OUR OWN GOOD: GOD'S RESPONSE TO ANGER

The Bible draws a clear parallel between God's anger and His love. In the Old Testament, He typically sent a prophet to proclaim to the people His displeasure with their evil deeds and to call them to repentance. If the people repented, God's anger subsided and all was well. However, if they did not repent, God took additional action. God's message to Jeremiah demonstrates this. "Go and give this message to Israel. This is what the LORD says: '. . . Come home to me again, for I am merciful. I will not be angry with you forever, Only acknowledge your guilt. . . . Return home, you wayward children' says the LORD, 'for I am your master'" (Jeremiah 3:12–14). Israel had forsaken truth and followed lies. God's anger motivated Him to send Jeremiah to call the people to repentance.

God took similar action in sending Jonah to Nineveh. The people of Nineveh knew God's reputation. When Jonah warned of the destruction in forty days, the Scriptures say, "The people of Nineveh believed God's message, and from the greatest to the least, they declared a fast and put on burlap to show their sorrow." Soon the king declared, "No one, not even the animals from your herds and flocks, may eat or drink anything at all. People and animals alike must wear garments of mourning, and everyone must pray earnestly to God. They must turn from their evil ways and stop all their violence. Who can tell? Perhaps even yet God will change his mind and hold back his fierce anger from destroying us." The people of Nineveh knew that God's anger was always driven by His love. So the Scriptures record, "When God saw what they had done and how they had put a stop to their evil ways, he changed his mind and did not carry out the destruction he had threatened" (Jonah 3:5, 7–10).

God's anger was expressed in positive action—declaring to the evildoer that all evil would be punished. Because of God's love for them, He could not allow injustice to go unpunished. However, when the people of Nineveh repented and turned from their evil ways, God's compassion moved Him to forgiveness. The wrong had been made right; God's anger had served its positive purpose.

Some contemporary students of the Bible have questioned God's severe acts of judgment on His people Israel and their neighbors. They have read into these acts the picture of a vengeful and destructive deity. However, upon closer examination, one discovers that when God used such drastic measures it was for the ultimate good of His creatures. His holiness will not allow God to remain silent when His children are involved in evil activity, and His love always seeks to express His anger for the larger good of humankind.

WHAT MADE JESUS ANGRY?

When we turn to the New Testament and examine the life of Jesus, we find that He too took positive, loving action against the evil that had stirred His anger. Perhaps the best known of these events was Jesus' experience in the temple in Jerusalem when He saw the merchants buying and selling oxen, sheep, and doves. He said, "The Scriptures declare, 'My Temple will be called a house of prayer,' but you have turned it into a den of thieves!" (Matthew 21:13). Much earlier in His ministry, Jesus had upbraided the moneychangers: "Stop turning my Father's house into a marketplace!" (John 2:16). John the apostle recorded that Jesus made a whip of cords, drove them from the temple area, and "scattered the money changers' coins over the floor, and turned over their tables" (verse 15).

Some would ask, "Where was Jesus' spirit of forgiveness?" We can without question assume that had the wrongdoers repented, He would have forgiven them. But remember, God's forgiveness is always in response to man's repentance. His action demonstrated not only to the merchants but also to the religious leaders that what was going on was inappropriate for the temple of God. In fact, John records, "His disciples remembered this prophecy from the Scriptures: 'Passion for God's house will consume me'" (2:17; see Psalm 69:9). The disciples clearly saw Jesus' anger being expressed, and they attributed it to His righteous and deep concern that His Father's house be a place of prayer rather than a place of merchandise.

On another occasion Jesus was in the synagogue on the Sabbath, and a man came to Him with a paralyzed hand. The Pharisees were looking for an occasion to accuse Jesus of breaking the Sabbath law, so Jesus asked the question, "Which is lawful on the Sabbath: to do good or to do evil, to save life or to kill?" The Pharisees remained silent, and Mark records that Jesus "looked around at them in anger and, deeply distressed at their stubborn hearts, said to the man, 'Stretch out your hand.' He stretched it out, and his hand was completely restored" (Mark 3:4–5 NIV). Jesus was angered by the Pharisees' legalistic thinking, which placed the keeping of Sabbath laws above ministry to human need. His action was to heal the man in front of their faces, rejecting their evil thinking and graphically demonstrating in front of everyone that human ministry is more important than religious observances.

Thus, the divine model is clear: God's response to anger is always to take loving action, to seek to stop the evil, and to redeem the evildoer.

A MOTHER'S RESPONSE TO A TERRIBLE WRONG

What about us? Because, as we have seen, we bear the image of God, each of us has on some level a concern for righteousness, fairness, and justice. Whenever we encounter that which we believe to be unrighteous, unkind, or unjust, we experience anger. I believe that in God's design *this anger is to motivate us to take positive, loving action to seek to set the wrong right*; and where there has been a relationship, to restore the relationship with the wrongdoer. Anger is not designed to drive us to do destructive things to the people who may have wronged us, nor does it give us license to say or do destructive things to our neighbors. *Anger's fundamental purpose is to motivate us to positive, loving action that will leave things better than we found them.*

> **JESUS WAS ANGERED BY THE PHARISEES' LEGALISTIC THINKING. HIS ACTION WAS TO HEAL THE MAN IN FRONT OF THEIR FACES.**

First, let us examine this in the whole area of social reform. Most readers will be familiar with the organization MADD (Mothers Against Drunk Drivers). Do you have any idea why this organization was established? I suggest to you that it was born out of anger. Mothers watched their sons and daughters being killed in the streets by drunken drivers. When these drivers came to trial, they were given a slap on the wrist, perhaps given a small fine, and returned to the streets the next day.

The mothers said, "This is not right." The founder, Candy Lightner, was shocked when a drunken driver plowed his vehicle into her thirteen-year-old daughter, leaving little Cari dead. Later her shock and grief turned into intense anger when a California judge gave the repeat-offender drunk driver a light sentence. She and other outraged mothers soon formed MADD. It was this anger, provoked by the injustice that they observed, that motivated Mrs. Lightner and other outraged mothers to establish a national organization that later grew to more than four hundred chapters.

Initially, their approach was to take turns sitting in the court-room when those who were charged with "driving under the influence" were being tried. They looked into the eyes of the judge, the lawyers, and the drunken drivers. Their presence moved judges to think twice before returning the license of a drunken driver. They also pressured state legislators to enact tougher laws against drunk driving. I don't think I have to tell you that the penalties for driving under the influence have become more stringent the last few years, and more drivers' licenses have been removed from those driving under the influence than ever before. All because some mothers got angry. MADD continues to seek judicial and legislative reforms.

The organization SADD (Students Against Driving Drunk) formed in a similar manner. Students were upset about the harm caused by drunken student drivers; they began to say, "It is not right to allow a fellow student to drive while under the influence of alcohol." These students began to organize, and committed themselves to have a designated, sober driver who would volunteer to drive the intoxicated students home. They took positive, loving action in response to their anger.

"TO LOOSE THE CHAINS OF INJUSTICE"

The abolition of slavery in England and America came about because a significant number of people felt anger about social conditions. The story of William Wilberforce, a great man of faith, wealthy Member of Parliament, and social reformer, is familiar to many. In 1807 Wilberforce and Thomas Clarkson persuaded the British government to pass a bill against the slave trade—but that victory was the culmination of a long, sometimes lonely battle. For decades previously, Wilberforce had waged a tireless crusade, delivering passionate speeches in Parliament detailing and decrying the evils of the slave trade. Across the ocean in the United States, a number of men and women looked at enslavement and said within their own hearts, *This is not right*. Years later the evil was officially ended when President Lincoln signed the Emancipation Proclamation. But it took people moved by anger at evil and injustice—people like Harriet Beecher Stowe, author of *Uncle Tom's Cabin*—to prick the conscience of a nation.

This is in keeping with God's desires as stated through the prophet Isaiah: "Free those who are wrongly imprisoned; lighten the burden of those who work for you. Let the oppressed go free, and remove the chains that bind people. Share your food with the hungry, and give shelter to the homeless. Give clothes to those who need them, and do not hide from relatives who need your help" (Isaiah 58:6–7).

But how does this work in everyday life?

Let's return to Brooke, whom we met in the last chapter. She is angry with her preschool children because of what she considers to be their inappropriate behavior, mad at her husband because he doesn't give her adequate help at home, mad at herself because she made the choice to be at home with her children, and ultimately mad at God, because in her mind He allowed her to get into this mess. At the moment, we are not concerned with what specific actions Brooke should take. We are simply asking, What is the purpose of Brooke's anger? I suggest that it is to motivate her to take positive, loving action to deal with what she considers to be unkind, inequitable, unfair, and inhumane. She is not to ignore her anger. Anger is like a red light flashing on the dash of a car. It indicates that something needs attention.

Anger can be a powerful and positive motivator, useful to move us toward loving action to right wrongs and correct injustice—but it also can become a raging, uncontrolled force.

So the difficulty is that all of these wonderfully positive purposes of anger seem to elude us in the heat of anger. We forget about setting things right and end up making things worse. This brings us to the next pressing question: How can we process anger in a positive way?

People who fly into a rage
always make a bad landing.

WILL ROGERS

CHAPTER 3

WHEN YOU'RE ANGRY FOR GOOD REASON

The following people all feel anger for different reasons. Yet the object of their anger is the same. Can you recognize what it is?

- Every time Monique attends a family gathering, she prays beforehand. Why? Because she knows her younger sister Felicia will "get on her case" about something: her hairstyle, her eating habits, or the way she treats their mother. Monique tries to maintain peace for her mother's sake, but inwardly she's furious.
- Ben is an independent consultant running his own business. One of his clients owes him a sizable amount. Ben has called, written, texted, emailed, and dropped by in person. The

client keeps promising, but the check is never in the mail. Ben is extremely angry and contemplating a lawsuit.

- Anna and Nate have been dating for months and are beginning to talk marriage. Anna loves Nate, but it bothers her that he invariably runs late. Now, as she waits for him to pick her up after work, she begins to feel the familiar irritation.

- Alan's neighbor Tony decided last week to begin landscaping his front yard. In the process of removing shrubs, he took out two that were on Alan's lot. When Alan saw the holes and his bushes gone, he was shocked and then angry. His wife, Marilyn, gets an earful when she arrives home from work.

- Christina is sitting in my office, distraught. "I don't understand it," she said. "Steve and I have been married for fourteen years, and we've had a good marriage. Now he tells me he doesn't love me anymore and that he's in love with someone else. How could he be in love with someone else? Just last week he made love to me. How could he do that if he's in love with someone else?"

All these people feel angry toward the same object: someone else. This is the kind of anger we are discussing in this chapter: anger toward someone with whom you have a relationship. It may be a family member, roommate, friend, work associate, neighbor—anyone with whom you have an ongoing relationship.

POSITIVE? LOVING?

In processing anger toward someone with whom you have a relationship, two questions are paramount: 1. Is my response *positive*—does it have the potential for dealing with the wrong and healing the relationship? 2. Is my response *loving*—is it designed for the benefit of the person at whom I am angry?

We're talking here about *valid* anger—that is, anger provoked by genuine wrongdoing on the part of the other person, as in the above examples. How then should Monique, Ben, and the others deal with their valid anger? I counsel a five-step process: (1) consciously acknowledge to yourself that you are angry; (2) restrain your immediate response; (3) locate the focus of your anger; (4) analyze your options; and (5) take constructive action. As we complete each step, we move toward making our anger productive.

"YES, I'M ANGRY!"

First, consciously acknowledge to yourself that you are angry. "That's obvious," you might reply. "Anyone would know that I am angry." Perhaps, but the question is, Are you *conscious* of your anger? Because the emotion of anger comes on so suddenly, often we are caught up in a verbal or physical response to the anger before ever consciously acknowledging what is going on inside of us. We are far more likely to make a positive response to our anger if we first acknowledge to ourselves that we are angry.

I suggest that you say the words out loud. "I am angry about this! Now what am I going to do?" Such a statement places the issues squarely on the table. You are now not only aware of your own anger, but you have distinguished for yourself the difference between your anger and the action you are going to take. You have set the stage for applying reason to your anger rather than simply being controlled by your emotions. This is an important first step in processing anger positively.

As simple as this may sound, some Christians have difficulty with this. All their lives they have been taught that anger is sin. Thus, to admit that they are angry is to admit that they are sinning. But this is not the biblical perspective on anger. I hope that the first two chapters have made it clear that the experience of anger is not sinful. It is a part of our humanity and reflects the anger experienced by God Himself. The apostle Paul stated it clearly when he said, "In your anger do not sin" (Ephesians 4:26 NIV). The challenge is not "Don't get angry"; the challenge is not to sin when we are angry.

That is precisely the topic we are addressing in this chapter. "How do I keep from sinning when I am angry?" Or to put it in a positive way, "How do I respond to my anger so that my actions will be constructive?" I believe that consciously and verbally acknowledging to yourself that you are angry is a first step in reaching this objective.

RESTRAINT: COUNTING TO 1,000

Second, restrain your immediate response. Very few adults have learned how to control and direct their anger. Most of us follow the patterns we learned in childhood by observing our parents or other significant adults. These patterns tend to cluster around two extremes: verbal or physical venting on the one hand, or withdrawal and silence on the other. Both are destructive.

THERE IS THAT MOMENT BEFORE THE RED-HOT WORDS BEGIN TO FLOW THAT WE CAN TRAIN OURSELVES TO RESTRAIN OUR ANGRY RESPONSE.

For most of us, anger control will be something we must learn as adults, and that means *unlearning* old habits. Thus, restraining our immediate response is extremely important in establishing new patterns. Restraining our response is not the same as storing our anger. It is refusing to take the action that we typically take when feeling angry. Solomon wisely wrote, "Fools vent their anger, but the wise quietly hold it back" (Proverbs 29:11). And again, "Sensible people control their temper" (Proverbs 19:11). Or consider the soberness of this proverb by Solomon: "Short-tempered people do foolish things" (14:17). Author Ambrose Bierce said, "Speak when you are angry and you will make the best speech you will ever regret." Most of us have had the experience of saying or doing things in the immediate flush of anger that we later regretted but unfortunately were unable to erase. Or perhaps we sent a scathing text or email to someone in the heat of the moment. Far better to learn to restrain our immediate response.

From time to time I meet people in my marriage seminars who say to me, "I cannot control my anger. When I get angry, I'm overwhelmed. I can't stop. I just go berserk." While I am sympathetic with what the person is saying, and I understand the overpowering nature of anger once it starts to roll, I believe that this is an ill-founded statement. It is true that once we begin to release anger in a destructive way verbally or physically, it's difficult to stop the flow of lava. But there is that moment before the red-hot words begin to flow that we can train ourselves to restrain that response.

Did your mother give you this commonsense advice? "When you're angry, count to ten before you do or say anything." It is good advice, but many of us may need to count to 100 or even 1,000. This long delay may quell the fire within. Many have found this to be a workable technique in helping them restrain their response.

I suggest that you count out loud. If you are in the presence of the person at whom you are angry, I suggest you leave. Take a walk as you count. About halfway around the block when you come to 597, you will probably be in a mental and emotional state where you can stop and say, "I am angry about this. Now what am I going to do?" For the Christian, this is the time to pray, "Lord, You know that I am angry. I believe that what they have done is wrong. Please help me make a wise decision about how to respond in this situation." Then with God you begin to look at your options.

Another technique that I have often shared in my marriage seminars is to call "time-out" when you realize that you are angry. This may be expressed verbally by simply saying the word "time-out," or it may be expressed visually by the time-out sign often seen in athletic events on television in which outstretched fingers on both hands are brought together to form a *T.* It is your symbol for saying, "I'm feeling angry right now and I don't want to lose it, so time-out." If both of you understand that this is a positive technique and not a cop-out on the situation, then you can accept this as a positive step in controlling anger. Please note that the time-out is not for three months; it is simply for a brief time to give you an opportunity to get in control of your emotions so that you can approach the situation with constructive action.

WHY ARE YOU REALLY ANGRY?

Step three takes place as you are restraining your immediate response. While you are on your "time-out" and after you have counted to 100—or 1,000—*locate the focus of your anger.* If you are angry with your spouse, ask yourself the following questions: Why am I so angry? Is it what my spouse has said or done? Is it the way he or she is talking? Is it the way he or she is looking at me? Does my spouse's behavior remind me of my mother or father? Is my anger toward my spouse influenced by something that happened at work today or in my childhood years ago?

Sheila was angry because her teenage son Josh neglected to clean his room before leaving the house—and her mother was due to arrive in three hours. After Josh had gone out and Sheila had time to cool down and reflect on the episode, she realized that her anger toward Josh was more about her mother than about her son. Her mind rushed back to a scene years ago in which her mother had glared at her and said, "You'll never amount to anything. Look, you can't even keep your room cleaned up." That same mother would soon walk through the door and observe Josh's room. Would this be the final evidence that Sheila was indeed a failure? She admitted that if her mother were not coming, Josh's room would not be a big deal to her. In fact, his room was often cluttered. This understanding helped Sheila take a more positive approach to her anger.

The bottom line in locating the focus of your anger is to discover the wrong committed by the person at whom you are angry. What is the person's sin? How has she wronged you? Doug angrily said of his wife, Kelly, "She never has any time for me! I wish someone would tell her that she's married." When he analyzed his anger, he realized that the issue was not whether Kelly should go out with her friends. His anger really focused on his unmet need for love. In his mind, that was the real issue. A wife should express love to her husband. He did not feel loved. He felt neglected. His anger really focused on Kelly's failure to meet his emotional need for love. This insight led him to process his anger in a much more constructive manner.

The secondary issue is, how serious is the offense? Nate not showing up on time for a date is certainly not on the same level as Nate being abusive. Some wrongs are minor and some are major. Each calls for a different response. To have the same response to minor issues as one does for major issues is to mismanage one's anger.

You may find it helpful to rate the seriousness of the issue on a scale of one to ten, with ten as the most serious of offenses and one as a minor irritation. Numbering the level of offense will not only help you get it in perspective, but sharing the number with the person at whom you are angry may prepare him or her mentally and emotionally to process the anger with you. If you tell me the issue is a "two," I will know that this will not take all night and that if I give you my full attention and seek to understand, we can solve this one rather easily. On the other hand, if you tell me it is a "ten," I know I'm in for a long evening and must postpone my book reading till another night.

CONFRONT—OR OVERLOOK?

Locating the focus of your anger and the seriousness of the offense prepares you for taking *step four: Analyze your options.* It is now time to ask the question, What are the possible actions I could take? You may want to write down the thoughts that come to your mind or verbalize them aloud to yourself.

The options are many. You could go back and give them a verbal berating because of their unjust, unkind, unloving, unthinking, uncaring behavior. You could also bring up all the past failures that come to your mind. You could even use curse words to show them how strongly you feel about the matter. You could go back and physically hit them over the head with a ball bat, slap them in the face, shake them vigorously, or throw a pop bottle at them. You might dismiss them with a mental putdown: *They're stupid, dumb, ignorant. I'm not going to waste my time even talking about the matter. It doesn't help to talk with an idiot. I'll just go to my computer room and never mention it again.* Or you might try for an element of revenge through isolation: *I will walk out of their lives and never see them again and never give them any further explanation. Let them experience rejection for a while.* These and many more options may flood your mind.

Which of these, if any, are prudent options? Well, remember our two fundamental questions: Is it positive and is it loving? That is, does the action I am considering have any potential for dealing with the wrong and helping the relationship? And is it best for the person at whom I am angry? It is my guess you will agree that most of the options we have noted above will not pass these tests. Theoretically they are options, but they are not constructive options. They are the kinds of things I may have done in the past, but they are not the kinds of things I want to do in the future.

What then are the Christian's options? As I see it, there are only two. One is to lovingly confront the person. The other is to consciously decide to overlook the matter. Let's look at the second option first. There are times when the best Christian option is to admit that I have been wronged but to conclude that confronting the person who did the wrong holds little or no redemptive value. Therefore, I choose to accept the wrong and commit the person to God. This is not the same as stuffing or storing your anger. It is quite the opposite. It is releasing the anger to God. It is giving up the right to take revenge, which, according to Scripture, is always God's prerogative (see Romans 12:19), and it is refusing to let what has happened eat away at your own sense of well-being. You are making a conscious choice to overlook the offense.

This is what the Bible calls *forbearance*, and it's turning the matter of justice over to God, knowing that He is totally aware of the situation. Thus, God can do to the individual whatever He judges to be wise. You are choosing not to be an emotional captive to the wrong that was perpetrated against you.

At times this option may be the best. For example, your parents have wronged you for many years or hurt you deeply on two or three counts at crucial periods in your life. You have had a surface relationship with them, but the anger has lived in your heart all these years. Perhaps you have now become a Christian or are now growing as a Christian, and you want to deal with this anger. You look at your parents, who are now in their eighties. You know in your heart that they are not capable of understanding or responding to the hurt that you have felt. You remember making an attempt on one occasion several years ago and getting nowhere. Thus, you decide it's time to let it go.

You may say, "I will never have the in-depth relationship I wish with my parents, but to confront them at this point would be counter-productive; therefore, I release my anger and hurt to God, knowing that He loves me with an unconditional love, knowing that He is both a just and merciful God and will do what is right by my parents." And then you say: "I release my parents to His care, and I release my anger and allow God's Holy Spirit to fill my being and cleanse me from all resentment and anger." You have consciously chosen the road of forbearance.

THE CHRISTIAN HAS TWO OPTIONS: TO LOVINGLY CONFRONT THE PERSON, OR TO DECIDE TO OVERLOOK THE MATTER.

Here's another instance where a forbearing response might

be best. Your supervisor at work has treated you unfairly. In the process of analyzing your anger and exploring your options, you remember that five of your friends have confronted the same supervisor in recent years—and each of them was summarily dismissed. Thus, you conclude that the supervisor is an uncaring, unreasonable individual, that talking with her would likely make things worse. Realizing that you have a family to support and that jobs are not readily available at the moment, you choose to let it go. You know that choosing to do so will not change your feelings or thoughts about the supervisor. You still feel the hurt, and you still perceive that you have been treated unfairly, but you make the conscious choice to let it go. Perhaps you begin looking for another job, or perhaps you will realize that to stay with the company means that you will likely not advance up the corporate ladder as long as your supervisor is with the company. In either case, you affirm that confronting the supervisor with your anger will again be counterproductive.

When taking such action, you release both the supervisor and your anger to God. To get on with your life, you deem those actions to be best. Doing so will not enhance your relationship with your supervisor, but at least it gives you the freedom to invest your emotional and physical energies in activities that are more productive.

There are many other occasions in which overlooking the offense may be the best option. The Scriptures acknowledge that this is often a valid way to handle one's anger. For example, "Fools vent their anger, but the wise quietly hold it back" (Proverbs 29:11). Our anger is released to God. The whole matter is placed in His hands, and we move on with our lives.

However, far more often the wise response to anger is to lovingly confront the person who has wronged you in an effort to seek reso-lution. "If another believer sins, rebuke that person; then if there is repentance, forgive" (Luke 17:3). Notice that Jesus is talking about those with whom you have a relationship. He says, "If another believer sins . . . against you." Furthermore, the word translated *to rebuke* means literally "to set a weight upon." Thus, to rebuke is to lay a matter before someone, to clearly bring it to the person's atten-tion. There are numerous examples of this in the New Testament.

On one occasion Jesus began to teach His disciples that He was going to suffer many things and be rejected by the elders and chief priests and that He would be killed and after three days He would rise again. The Scriptures record the reaction of one disciple: "Peter took him aside and began to rebuke him" (Mark 8:32 NIV). Why did Peter rebuke Jesus? Because in his mind, what Jesus was saying was wrong. *This is not the way you establish a kingdom. And certainly my Master is not going to be killed.* Perhaps Peter thought Jesus was depressed, but he certainly didn't agree with what Jesus was saying, so he privately rebuked Him.

In response, "Jesus turned and looked at his disciples." Then "he rebuked Peter. 'Get behind me, Satan!' he said. 'You do not have in mind the concerns of God, but merely human concerns'" (Mark 8:33 NIV). Jesus knew that Peter misunderstood reality; that in fact he was speaking the words of Satan. In brief, Peter was wrong, and Jesus clearly confronted him with his wrong. On another occasion, Jesus rebuked James and John for their hostile attitude toward the unbe-lieving Samaritans. They suggested, "'Lord, should we call down fire from heaven to burn them up?' But Jesus turned and rebuked them. So they went on to another village" (Luke 9:54–56). Clearly their attitude was wrong, and Jesus brought the matter to their attention.

Rebuke is not verbal abuse. Rebuke is laying a matter before a brother or sister whom you perceive to have wronged you. Such a rebuke needs to be done kindly and firmly, recognizing that there is always a possibility that we have misunderstood the brother's words or actions as Peter misunderstood the words of Jesus regarding the Savior's approaching death.

I often suggest that people write their rebuke before trying to speak it. It may go something like this: "I've got something that has been bothering me. In fact, I guess I would have to say I'm feeling angry. Perhaps I am misunderstanding the situation, but when you have an opportunity, I'd like to talk with you about it."

Such a statement reveals where you are, openly reveals your anger, and requests an opportunity to process it with the person involved. You have acknowledged up front that your perception may be imperfect, but at any rate, you want to get the issue resolved. Few people will not respond with an opportunity to talk about it if you approach them in such a manner. If given the opportunity, then you lay before them your perception of what you heard or saw or think to be true, and ask if you are understanding the situation correctly. This gives the person an opportunity to (1) share with you information that you may not be aware of, or (2) explain his motives in what he did or said, or (3) clearly admit to you that what he did was wrong and to ask your forgiveness.

In this context of open communication, each trying to understand the other, the issue will be resolved. Either by the other's explanation or the other's confession of wrong, the framework is laid for reconciliation. If the person admits to wrongdoing and expresses a repentant attitude, the clear teaching of Jesus is that we are to forgive the individual.

In Matthew 18:15–17, Jesus described how this principle works in the context of the local church. "If another believer sins against you, go privately and point out the offense. If the other person listens and confesses it, you have won that person back. But if you are unsuccessful, take one or two others with you and go back again, so that everything you say may be confirmed by or three witnesses. If the person still refuses to listen, take your case to the church. Then if he or she won't accept the church's decision, treat that person as a pagan or a corrupt tax collector." And how do you treat a pagan or a tax collector? You pray for his salvation and you pray for his restoration. You treat the person with dignity and respect, as an individual for whom Christ died. But you cannot have warm fellowship with him because he refuses to deal with the offense, which always divides.

Thus, in the church or out of the church, reconciliation with a friend or family member is always the ideal. Confronting is never for the purpose of condemning but rather for restoring the relationship to one that is genuine, open, and loving. If there has been a misunderstanding, the air is to be cleared so that we can resume fellowship as brothers or husband and wife. If wrongdoing is confessed, we are to forgive and the relationship is restored. The apostle Paul wrote that we must always remember that next time we may be the one who offends (see Galatians 6:1). None of us is perfect, and when we do wrong, we are likely to stimulate anger in the person whom we have wronged.

Loving confrontation is not easy for most people. We have had no training and very little experience in this approach to handling anger. We are far more experienced in either ventilating or seeking to deny or hide our anger, but such approaches are always destructive. Loving confrontation with a view to reconciliation is normally the best approach.

THE FINAL STEP: TAKE CONSTRUCTIVE ACTION

Which brings us to our *fifth step: Take constructive action.* Once we have explored our options, it is time to take action. If I choose to let the offense go, then I should share this decision with God. You might say something like this: "Lord, You know what has happened. You know how hurt I am, how angry I feel. But I really believe that the best thing for me to do in this situation is to accept the wrong and turn the person over to You. You know not only his actions but his motives. I know that You are a righteous God, so I trust You to do what is right by the person. I also release my anger to You. The anger moved me to think through the situation, and I am taking the step I believe to be best. Therefore, the matter is over. My anger has served its purpose, and I release it to You. Help me not to be controlled by any residual thoughts and feelings that come to me over the next few days. I want to use my life constructively and not be hindered by this event. Thank You that I am Your child and You will take care of me."

CONFRONTING IS NEVER FOR THE PURPOSE OF CONDEMNING.

If over the next few days or weeks your mind reverts to the wrong done to you, and the emotions of hurt and anger return, take those thoughts and feelings to God and say, "Lord, You know what I am remembering right now, and You know the feelings that I am feeling. But I thank You that I have dealt with that, and I release these thoughts and feelings to You. Help me now to do something constructive with my life the rest of this day." Then you move out to face the challenges of today.

On the other hand, if you choose the option of lovingly confronting the person who has wronged you, remember the challenge given by Paul. "Brothers and sisters, if another believer is overcome by some sin, you who are godly should gently and humbly help that person back onto the right path. And be careful not to fall into the same temptation yourself" (Galatians 6:1). Your confrontation may go something like this: "I have something that is bothering me, and I need your input. Is there a time we can talk?"

If your request is granted, you may say something like, "I'm feeling some hurt and anger over something that happened. I know that I may be misunderstanding the situation. That's why I want to talk about it. Yesterday when you [whatever], I interpreted that as a very unkind action. I felt like you were not considering my feelings at all. Maybe I misunderstood your actions, but I need to resolve this." Perhaps the person will give an explanation that will shed light upon his or her actions and give you a different perspective on the actions and the person's intentions. On the other hand, the person may admit that what he or she did was thoughtless and unkind and may ask you to forgive him or her. In this case, you must always forgive.

If the offense was extremely grave in nature, forgiveness may not restore your trust in the person. We will discuss the nature of forgiveness in a later chapter, but forgiveness is the promise that you will no longer hold this particular offense against the person. Your anger has served its purpose, and the two of you are reconciled.

Such loving confrontation typically results in either a genuine confession of wrongdoing and the extending of forgiveness, or the conversation sheds new light upon the subject; you learn that what the person said or did was not exactly what you had perceived or that the motives were not the ones that you had attributed to him or her. In either case, the issue is cleared; the matter is resolved and the relationship continues to grow. Anger has served its rightful purpose. It has motivated you to take constructive action to see that the issue was resolved.

"I DON'T WANT MONEY TO COME BETWEEN US"

Confrontation does not always lead to justice, but it may well lead to a restored relationship. Nick, a hardworking entrepreneur, had achieved some success in his business and had accumulated a substantial investment portfolio. Jerry, his longtime friend, was starting a new business and came to Nick asking for a loan of $50,000 to help him get his business off the ground. Nick freely loaned him the money. They each signed a simple loan agreement that Jerry could have the money for one year without interest and after that would repay the entire sum or renegotiate the loan.

By the end of the year, Jerry's business was no longer in existence, and the $50,000 had been spent. Jerry got another job, but his salary was not adequate to repay the loan. He promised to repay Nick whenever he was able over the next five years. Jerry never made enough to repay the loan. He had good intentions but never came through with the money. Nick let it ride but struggled with anger toward Jerry.

Eventually Nick had a reversal in his own business and could really have used the $50,000, but Jerry was not able to pay. After much prayer and talking with his pastor and other trusted advisors, he confronted Jerry and shared his anger. Jerry expressed his own pain that he had not been able to repay the loan. "If I had the money,

I would give it to you," he said. "If I ever get it, I will give it to you."

Nick decided to no longer expect the money from Jerry. He told Jerry, "We've been friends for a long time. I don't want money to be a barrier between us. If you are ever able to repay the loan, I would really like that, but if not, I'm not going to pressure you over the money."

Nick had the legal right to sue Jerry for failure to repay. However, he knew that to do so would devastate Jerry financially. He chose not to do that, believing that it would serve no good purpose. His was the choice to accept less than he desired. He and Jerry are still friends, and Jerry is grateful for Nick's attitude and sincerely hopes that someday he will be able to repay his old friend.

There are times when choosing not to seek justice is the best alternative. For Nick, this was a conscious choice that came after confronting Jerry with his thoughts and feelings. Confrontation led to a resolution that was something less than ideal. But Nick is now free from his anger, and his relationship with Jerry has improved.

Of course, there is always the possibility that when you confront someone the person will deny wrongdoing, even though you know the person has wronged you. This often happens when a spouse confronts a partner who is guilty of having an affair. The partner lies in order to protect himself or herself. The lie itself gives rise to more anger. If you are certain of your facts, you must then realize that you cannot reconcile with this person. Unconfessed sin fractures relations with people and God. You must then decide what your next step will be. This may be turning to a pastor, counselor, or trusted friend to seek advice. It may be reading an appropriate book. It will certainly mean prayer for God's guidance in what you should do.

If after further confrontation the person refuses to deal with his wrongdoing, you must eventually acknowledge that the person is choosing not to continue his relationship with you. We cannot make people confess, repent, and reconcile with us. We must let them walk away, and we must pray for them. Loving confrontation does not always result in reconciliation, but it does give us the peace of mind that we sought to deal with the wrong in a responsible manner.

In summary, here are the steps in responding to anger:

1. Consciously acknowledge to yourself that you are angry.
2. Restrain your immediate response.
3. Locate the focus of your anger.
4. Analyze your options.
5. Take constructive action.

This is the road to making anger productive—and it is worth spending some time reflecting on and praying about these steps, or even jotting them in a journal if you are so inclined. You will also find some pointers on these five steps in the summary "Quick Takes" (next page).

HOW TO HANDLE YOUR ANGER

1. Consciously acknowledge to yourself that you are angry. Say it out loud: "I'm angry about this! Now what am I going to do?" Such a statement makes you aware of your own anger and also helps you recognize both your anger and the action you are going to take. You have set the stage for applying reason to your anger.

2. Restrain your immediate response. Avoid the common but destructive responses of verbal or physical venting or their opposite, withdrawal and silence. Refuse to take the action that you typically take when feeling angry. Waiting can help you avoid both saying and doing things you may not mean and later will regret.

3. Locate the focus of your anger. What words or actions by the other person have made you angry? If the person has truly wronged you, identify the person's sin. How has she wronged you? Then determine how serious the offense is. Some wrongs are minor and some are major. Knowing its seriousness should affect your response.

4. Analyze your options. Ask yourself: Does the action I am considering have any potential for dealing with the wrong and helping the relationship? And is it best for the person at whom I am angry? The two most constructive options are either to confront the person in a helpful way, or to consciously decide to overlook the matter.

5. Take constructive action. If you choose to "let the offense go," then, in prayer, confess your anger and your willingness to turn the person over to God. Then release your anger to Him. If you choose to confront the person who has wronged you, do so gently. Listen to any explanation; it can give you a different perspective on the person's actions and intentions. If the person admits that what he or she did was wrong and asks you to forgive, do so.

"Anger" is one letter short
of "danger."

AUTHOR UNKNOWN

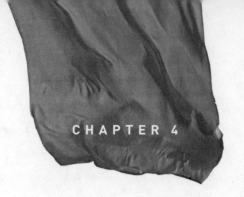

CHAPTER 4

WHEN ANGER IS WRONG

By this time you may be asking, "If anger is so positive, then why has it caused so much trouble in the world?"

The answer is as ancient as the garden of Eden. The drama revealed in Genesis 3 featuring Adam and Eve, the serpent, and a fruit tree significantly altered human nature. We now have the tendency to take every good gift of God and distort it into something perverse. The gifts of reason, sexuality, love, and so much more have all been perverted.

Anger is no different. The deceiver is still among us, and the scene of Eden is repeated daily. Perverting the divine purpose of anger has been one of Satan's most successful tactical designs.

The Enemy has used many strategies to twist God's intention for human anger. One of the most powerful is to make us think that *all* of our anger is of equal value: "If I perceive that I have been wronged, then I have been wronged." This illusion leads us to conclude that we always have a right to feel angry.

DEFINITIVE OR DISTORTED?

But the fact is that much of our anger is distorted. Two kinds of anger exist: *definitive* and *distorted.* Definitive anger is born of wrongdoing. Someone treats us unfairly, steals our property, lies about our character, or in some other way does us wrong. This is the only kind of anger God ever experiences. It is valid anger. The second kind of anger, however, is *not* valid. It is triggered by a mere disappointment, an unfulfilled desire, a frustrated effort, a bad mood, or any number of other things that have nothing to do with any moral transgression. The situation simply has made life inconvenient for us, touched one of our emotional hot spots, or happened at a time when we were extremely tired or stressed.

I call this "distorted anger," not because the emotions are any less intense than those experienced with definitive anger, but because they are the responses to something less than genuine wrongdoing. Much of our anger with people is also distorted. What the person did frustrated me, disappointed me, hurt me, or embarrassed me, but what the person did was not actually wrong. My anger experience may be just as intense as ever, but my response to such anger will be different from my response to definitive anger.

THE STORY OF A VALIANT SOLDIER

That people can recognize when anger is distorted and make positive responses is illustrated by the story of Naaman, a great military commander and valiant soldier who had leprosy. The commander had heard from a young girl, a prisoner of war, that a prophet in Israel could heal leprosy. Naaman immediately went to the king, told him what the young girl had said, and asked permission to go to the prophet in Israel. The king not only gave permission but encouraged Naaman in his pursuit. Naaman packed his gold, silver, and other gifts and headed off in search of healing. When, through a circuitous route, he finally reached the gate that led to the prophet's house, the prophet did not so much as go to the door. Rather, he sent a messenger, saying to Naaman, "Go, wash yourself seven times in the Jordan, and your flesh will be restored and you will be cleansed." Naaman's response is notable:

> But Naaman became angry and stalked away. "I thought he would certainly come out to meet me!" he said. "I expected him to wave his hand over the leprosy and call on the name of the Lord his God and heal me! Aren't the rivers of Damascus, the Abana and the Pharpar, better than any of the rivers of Israel? Why shouldn't I wash in them and be healed?" So Naaman turned and went away in a rage. (2 Kings 5:11–12)

Clearly, Naaman is an angry man. His blood pressure has risen. His nostrils are flared. His feet are stamping the dry ground. His anger quickly jumps to rage. Thoughts, which to him seem logical, race through his mind. *How absurd, how foolish. Where is the respect? I'm giving him a chance to show his God's power, and he tells me to go wash in the muddy Jordan. How ridiculous.*

In Naaman's mind, Elisha the prophet has done him wrong. He has a right to be angry. Instead, the prophet has actually given him a cure for his leprosy. Elisha has done him great good, but because Naaman's thinking is distorted, he is experiencing anger toward the prophet. In his rage, he is ready to return to his homeland, his mission not only a failure but a great embarrassment.

Fortunately, there were some straight-thinking people traveling with him. His servants went to him and said,

"Sir, if the prophet had told you to do something very difficult, wouldn't you have done it? So you should certainly obey him when he says simply, 'Go and wash and be cured!'" So Naaman went down to the Jordan River and dipped himself seven times, as the man of God had instructed him. And his skin became as healthy as the skin of a young child, and he was healed!

Then Naaman and his entire party went back to find the man of God. They stood before him, and Naaman said, "Now I know that there is no God in all the world except in Israel. So please accept a gift from your servant." (verses 13–15)

Elisha refused his gift but acknowledged the healing power of God.

Naaman represents the person who experiences strong but distorted anger but who, when confronted, stops his rage and listens to reason rather than allowing anger to control his behavior. As a result, this leader experienced healing and turned to honor the person at whom he had earlier been angry. Naaman demonstrates that distorted anger does not need to control our behavior and lead us to destructive acts.

This biblical account gives us a positive example of how to respond to distorted anger. This raises two questions: (1) How do we identify when our anger is distorted? (2) How do we process distorted anger? The first question is easier to answer, and we'll address it here. However, processing distorted anger is more challenging, and we'll answer that in the next chapter.

WRONGDOING—OR NOT?

Distorted anger differs from definitive anger in one fundamental way. In definitive anger, there is always a wrong perpetrated; the anger is a response to this wrong. In distorted anger, a *perceived* wrong leads to anger—but the alleged wrong is only in your perception; there is no real wrongdoing.

For instance, you are walking down the street and observe a teenage boy walk up to a younger and smaller boy, snatch his bicycle from his grip, and ride off down the street. The young boy is screaming, "That's my bike! That's my bike! He stole my bike!" Immediately you experience anger. Your emotions rise. Your heart rate quickens. Your mind begins to race: *The very idea of bullying around a younger child. That's not right! Something needs to be done.* If the facts are what you perceive them to be, then your anger is definitive.

But let's assume that upon further investigation, you find that the bicycle actually belonged to the older boy, that the younger boy saw it unattended and decided to take a ride. When the older boy spotted him, he was simply retrieving his bicycle before the young boy got out of sight. Your anger toward the older boy is distorted in that he perpetrated no wrong. In fact, he was correcting a wrong that had been committed by the younger boy. Distorted anger is based upon a perception of wrong, whereas definitive anger is based upon genuine wrong.

It becomes apparent that if we treat all anger as definitive, we will make some serious blunders in judgment. For example, if, in the above illustration, you assume that your anger is definitive, you may chase the older teen, knock him from the bicycle, and return it to the younger child. Only later will you realize that you have made a serious mistake.

In order to understand distorted anger, we must return to our basic paradigm. In all anger there is first a provoking event; second, an interpretation of that event; and third, the rising emotion of anger. Physiological changes take place in the body, and we are ready for action. All of this occurs whether the anger is definitive or distorted. But if we are to have a wise response to anger, we must first discern whether that anger is based upon actual wrongdoing. This requires time and thought. Thus, the value of step two in the last chapter: Restrain your immediate response. Questions must be asked and evidence must be weighed in order to process anger positively. These questions must be asked of yourself and sometimes of the other person.

MUCH OF OUR ANGER GROWS OUT OF INTERNAL EMOTIONAL AND THINKING PATTERNS THAT HAVE DEVELOPED THROUGH THE YEARS.

In the illustration above, had you raced to the younger child and asked, "Is that your bicycle?" he may have said, "No, I was just borrowing it for a short ride." Immediately you know that things are not exactly what you perceive them to be. With only one bit of new information, your anger is already beginning to subside. With the additional information, you may decide that no action toward the older boy needs to be taken, and you may end up giving the younger boy a lecture on not taking bicycles without permission. That's a much different action than you would have taken if you assumed your original anger to be definitive. (Of course, if you heard different stories from the two boys, any action is difficult. You may assume one is lying. The solution may be to go home with one of the boys and talk with his parents.)

Two questions are important in determining the validity of anger. The first is, What wrong was committed? And the second is, Am I sure I have all the facts?

The first question strikes at the heart of the matter. If a genuine wrong has been committed, then your anger is definitive. If, however, your anger has been born out of some unrealistic expectation inside of you, then it must be handled as distorted anger. Much of our anger grows out of internal emotional and thinking patterns that have developed through the years. For example, the person who tends to be a perfectionist will have high expectations not only for himself but for others to whom he relates. When people do not live up to these expectations, he will likely experience anger. Such anger is often distorted anger because the person has committed no wrong.

Jill is highly perfectionistic. Open the drawer of her dresser and you find all of her clothes neatly stacked and color-coordinated. Her closet is no less organized. This pattern for neatness and perfection appears in every aspect of her life. She is married to Jeff, who is highly creative, but neatness and organization are not even in his vocabulary. Jill often becomes angry when she observes Jeff's dirty clothes stuffed in a closet corner; when she sees him looking for a report he completed two weeks ago but has misplaced; and when she gets inside his car, which hasn't been cleaned since the day he brought it home from the dealer.

But Jeff has committed no wrong; Jeff is being the person Jeff has learned to be. He has no inner compulsion toward neatness or organization such as Jill has. I am not suggesting that Jill's anger is not real. It has the same emotional, physical, and cognitive aspects as definitive anger. She really is upset; she really believes that Jeff is wrong not to be neat. But if she is open to the facts, she will discover that thousands of people have Jeff's personality traits and that these traits are not evil. Jill's anger still needs to be processed in a positive way (we'll come to that in the next chapter), but it will help if she can see it for what it is. Her anger is not born out of Jeff's wrong-doing but out of her own compulsion for neatness and organization. If she can see it as distorted anger, she is far more likely to process it in a positive way.

Sometimes examining our anger will lead us to question the person with whom we are angry. If we understand that we may not have all the facts, then we should be motivated to seek the facts before we jump to wrong conclusions.

When we begin to examine anger, we will find that much of it falls into the category of distorted anger. Distorted anger is no less troublesome than definitive anger, but it needs to be processed in a different way. In chapter 5 we will consider how to process our distorted anger.

"GOOD" VERSUS "BAD" ANGER

"GOOD" (DEFINITIVE)

Definition: Anger toward any kind of genuine wrongdoing; mistreatment, injustice, breaking of laws

Sparked by: Violation of laws or moral code

How to recognize: If you can answer yes to the questions, Was a wrong committed? and Do I have all the facts?

What to do: Either confront the person or decide to overlook the offense (see chapter 3, step four).

"BAD" (DISTORTED)

Definition: Anger toward a *perceived* wrongdoing where no wrong occurred

Sparked by: People who hurt us; stress; fatigue; unrealistic expectations

How to recognize: Feelings of frustration or disappointment feed the anger.

What to do: Halt the anger, and gather information to process your anger.

For every minute you are angry you lose sixty seconds of happiness.

RALPH WALDO EMERSON

CHAPTER 5

HOW TO HANDLE "BAD" ANGER

Lynn was smoldering. Her daughter, Emily, had admitted to her that she was getting Cs and even a D at college. As they talked on the phone, Lynn had to bite her lip to keep from screaming: "But your dad and I sent you to this wonderful Christian college! I loved college! I wish I could take some of the classes you're taking! Do you know what we're paying?"

To Lynn, Emily's poor performance almost felt like a slap in the face. But her anger was distorted—based on a *perceived* injustice. In this case, Lynn's expectations fed her anger toward Emily.

Many of us struggle with these wrong perceptions that feed our resentment. Such distorted anger is sparked by such factors as circumstantial evidence, faulty presuppositions, generalizations, our expectations or personal preferences, even plain tiredness—and sometimes a combination of these. Whatever the cause, we conclude incorrectly that we have been wronged. We have an anger that is not valid, definitive anger; it's mistaken, distorted anger.

We have emphasized that distorted anger is wrong, and that it is a direct outcome of Adam and Eve's fall, arising out of our selfish, even prideful natures. But that does not rid us of our feelings as we are experiencing anger. So how do we address such anger—and channel it for the good?

"I NEED YOUR HELP": SHARING INFORMATION

We begin by telling the other person our point of concern. This must always be done in a nonjudgmental manner. That's why I am calling it "sharing information." We are not sharing a verdict: "You let me down"; "You disappointed me"; "You didn't do what you promised." All of these are condemning, judgmental statements that tend to incite warfare. In contrast, "I'm feeling frustrated (disappointed, hurt, angry, or any other emotion), and I need your help" is a statement of information. It's telling the other person what's going on inside of you, and it is requesting an opportunity to talk.

Sharing information rather than judgment is the first step in processing distorted anger. In sharing information, you are focusing on making the other person aware of your emotions, your thoughts, and your concerns. You are focusing on the event that provoked your feelings, not on the person. You are more likely to be able to do this if you have first determined that the person has not wronged you. He may have made your life difficult; he may have caused you frustration, but he has not committed an immoral act.

"WHAT HAPPENED?":
GATHERING INFORMATION

Earlier we noted that on some occasions, we will recognize that we don't have all the facts. Therefore, it is difficult for us to determine whether our anger is definitive or not. Meredith and Jason have a quick dinner, and she dashes out the door to attend her evening class. Three hours later, she returns home to find Jason on the couch watching a movie, the dirty dishes still sitting on the table where they left them. Meredith goes into an "anger attack." Thoughts race through her mind. *I can't believe this—watching a stupid movie for hours, and the mess just sits there while I've been working hard in class. The ants have probably cleaned the plates by now. I feel like going in there and kicking the television.*

Meredith has several options. She can conclude that her anger is legitimate, that her husband is a no-good, lazy slob, and she can respond to him with bitter words; she can withdraw in silence and be unresponsive to his efforts toward sexual intimacy later that evening; or she can try to handle her anger in a more responsible manner. If she understands the difference between definitive and distorted anger, she may begin by asking herself, *What wrong has he committed?* She may work hard in her mind to see his action (or inaction) as some sin. If she is successful, she may conclude that his sin is in not loving her. *After all, aren't husbands supposed to love their wives as Christ loved the church? Well, this is certainly not an expression of love.*

If she is wise, she will also ask herself, *Do I have all the facts?* If she is wise enough to ask the question, she will probably be wise enough to conclude that the answer is no, she does not have all the facts. Therefore, an important step is to get information from Jason as to what has happened and why.

Meredith walks over to the couch, sits down, gives Jason a kiss, and says, "I have one small question before I give you another kiss," she says. "Why are the dirty plates still on the table?"

"Oh, Babe, I'm sorry," Jason answers. "I sat down here to watch a movie. I meant to clean up when it was over, but the next thing I knew you were unlocking the door. I don't know how long I slept. I even slept through all the explosions in the film. I must have been asleep for two hours.

"I'll get the dishes. I'm sorry. I must have been exhausted." He stands, stretches, and goes to the kitchen to begin to clean up. "How was your class?" he says.

Chances are Meredith's anger begins to subside as she realizes that Jason's failure to clean up the table was not a sinful act. Sleeping for two hours on the couch is not immoral; it is simply a sign of one's humanity. Gathering information allowed Meredith to release her anger and perhaps even be glad that Jason was able to get some extra sleep.

When we realize that our perception of the situation is distorted, we can release that distorted anger and work on accepting our spouses as human.

"THIS REALLY BOTHERS ME": NEGOTIATING UNDERSTANDING

Sometimes even when our anger is distorted we cannot simply release it and accept what the other person has done. Often we need to negotiate understanding. For even when the other has done nothing morally wrong, his or her behavior is still painful. You still feel disappointed, frustrated, hurt, and angry. You need to understand the person's actions —and he or she needs to understand your feelings.

This requires open conversation in a nonjudgmental atmosphere. Understanding that the other person has not morally wronged you should help you approach them in a non-condemning way.

Rita and Doug are in their late thirties. They both have vocations that they find fulfilling. However, Rita has been struggling with anger toward Doug during the past six months. All of a sudden, he has become health-conscious. Three evenings a week after dinner, he goes to the local gym to work out, leaving her with the chores and the kids. He comes home later and wants her to watch television with him and, to use his words, "make love" with him. She is finding her anger growing into resentment. She feels that he is neglecting his responsibilities to help the children with their homework on those three nights. Rita's anger is growing daily. She feels as if she is about to explode. Doug seems to be happy, but she is extremely unhappy.

EVEN WHEN THE OTHER PERSON HAS DONE NOTHING MORALLY WRONG, THEIR BEHAVIOR CAN STILL BE PAINFUL.

When Rita expressed her anger to me in the counseling office, we began by trying to identify the specific things about Doug's behavior that sparked her anger. We came up with the following list:

- Doug is unfair to leave me with the chores while he goes off to have fun.
- He is neglecting the children by not helping them with their homework on those three nights.

- He is self-centered in that he expresses almost no interest in meeting my needs. In fact, I'm not sure he even understands what my needs are.

When we explored her needs, we found that her primary love language—the way she really felt loved by her husband—was quality time; the thing she really wanted from Doug was time together. "We used to talk a lot," she said. "I felt close to him; I felt like he cared. Now with him gone three nights a week, we just don't have time to talk. I'm beginning to feel he doesn't want to be with me."

We then turned our attention toward determining if her anger was distorted in these three areas. We looked at him leaving her with the dirty dishes three nights a week and I asked, "What wrong is he committing?"

"I just feel like it's unfair for him to walk out and leave me with the work. We both work outside the home. I work as hard as he does," she said.

"Does he help you around the house in other ways?" I inquired.

"Yes, actually he does a lot around the house. He takes care of the yard and all the outside work. He also vacuums for me. And he'll pitch in and help me with anything I ask him to do."

Then we turned to the matter of homework. "On the two nights that Doug does not go to the gym, does he help the children with their homework?"

"Yes," she said. "He always has. In fact, he used to help them every night. He still helps them a little bit when he gets home from the gym if there is something they're having trouble with. But it's not the same as it used to be."

"What was your life like before Doug started going to the gym three nights a week?"

"We would eat together unless the kids had a school activity, and then we would just grab a bite. He would always help me with the dishes. Then he and I would sit down and talk for probably thirty minutes before he helped the children with their homework and I worked on other things around the house. It was great. I felt close to him. I felt like we were a family. Now I feel like we're still a family, but he abandons us three nights a week."

When I asked if her husband knew about her feelings toward his gym nights, she thought not, but then she added, "I feel like he is neglecting me and that we are growing apart. . . . He just doesn't realize what's happening."

As I questioned Rita further, she explained that Doug began to go to the gym after watching a video on fitness at his workplace and a coworker invited him to work out with him. She admitted, "I'm glad he's taking care of himself. I'm sure he feels better. I probably should be working out myself, but I just don't have time. I don't think he has time either, but he's making time. But it's at our expense, as I see it."

It seemed apparent to me that Doug's behavior did not fall into the category of immoral. What he was doing was not innately wrong. However, Rita had held on to her anger far too long. She needed to negotiate understanding. She needed to share with Doug what was going on inside of her—her thoughts, her feelings, her frustrations—not in a condemning manner but as information. And she needed to find out from Doug how he perceived these things; she needed to get information. But beyond that, this couple needed to come to a place of understanding, to find a way to meet all of their needs, and to help them reconnect with each other emotionally.

I suggested that Rita request of Doug a time to talk and that she begin by saying something like the following: "I know that you love me and you are a good husband. What I want to share with you is not designed in any way to put you down. But I want our relationship to be open and genuine, and I feel that I must share with you some of the struggles that I'm having. Over the past few months, I've sometimes felt hurt, disappointed, and neglected. A lot of it focuses around you going to the gym three nights a week.

"Please understand that I'm not against your efforts to stay in shape. I'm not even asking you to change that. I just want to share with you my struggles. My feelings focus on three specific areas. One, I feel that the kids are being neglected in terms of your helping them with their homework. I know that you still help them at night, but I have a concern that they're not getting all the help they need. Secondly, I feel like it's unfair that you get up from the dinner table and leave me to clean up on those three nights. And probably my biggest struggle is that I feel like I'm being neglected, that we don't have time to talk like we used to talk. Sometimes, I even feel like you don't want to talk with me, and I'm feeling a lot of distance between us. I felt it was unfair not to tell you about this because I need your help and your understanding."

My efforts were to help Rita share her struggles in a non-condemning manner, requesting understanding. That is my recommendation to anyone who, having recognized distorted anger and received information, needs to negotiate understanding. Sit down and express your need for understanding in a nonthreatening way.

Then I encouraged Rita to listen to Doug's response; not to try to counter what he said but rather to understand what he said. Then together they could seek to discover a way to meet her need for quality time with him, his need for physical fitness, the children's need for help with the homework, and her need for a feeling of equity in household responsibilities.

A month later Rita returned, and I was thrilled to hear that Doug had responded positively. In their conversation, he had assured her of his love; he agreed that together they would ask the children if they felt they were getting enough help with their homework, and if not, he was willing to make adjustments. He readily agreed to help her clean up the table before he went to the gym. He had not realized that this was a problem with her, and he agreed that they would make time for the two of them. In fact, for the past few weeks, they had been having lunch together two days a week, and he had arranged for a weekend away just for the two of them. If necessary, he was willing to cut back on his time at the gym, but Rita hesitated to encourage this after she saw Doug's positive response to her concerns.

MOST HUSBANDS WILL RESPOND POSITIVELY TO HIS WIFE'S REQUEST THAT HE SHAVE BEFORE GOING TO THE SUPERMARKET ON A SATURDAY, ESPECIALLY IF SHE FIRST AFFIRMS HER LOVE FOR HIM AND SAYS SHE ONLY WANTS HIM TO LOOK HIS BEST.

Negotiating understanding is an important part of human relationships, whether the relationship be in the family, church, vocation, or any other area. All of us feel better about our relationships when we negotiate understanding. Even distorted anger indicates that something needs attention. Such anger seldom dissipates without open, loving communication between the parties involved.

REQUESTING CHANGE

In all human relationships, people will find certain behavioral characteristics irritating. Though the particular behaviors may differ, the resulting irritations often stir anger within us. For the most part, this anger is distorted in that the other person's behavior is not morally wrong; he or she has not perpetrated an evil against us. If the relationship is a close relationship and the person is one with whom we spend a great deal of time, such as in family or vocation, it is sometimes helpful to seek to mitigate these irritations by requesting change. Please notice I say *requesting*, not demanding or manipulating. None of us responds well to those approaches.

However, if we have a generally positive relationship, most of us tend to respond well to requests. For example, here's an irritation that causes you anger in the workplace: Your colleague in the next cubicle tends to slurp her coffee while you are talking to a client in yours. You hear the sounds through the door and find it to be very offensive. After affirming her worth as a colleague, it is perfectly appropriate to request that she not drink coffee while you are seeing a client or that she learn to drink it silently. Chances are that a simple request will alleviate the source of your frustration and anger, especially if you make it clear that you are also open to her requests.

The same principle applies in marriage and family relationships. Assuming a fairly good relationship, most husbands will respond to his wife's request that he shave before going to the supermarket on a Saturday, especially if she makes her request after affirming her love for him and assuring him that her motive is that he look his best. Most wives will respond to the request to put their toiletries in a vanity drawer rather than littering the counter with them—if the husband makes his request after pointing out some positive traits about her and expressing his appreciation for all the other things that she does.

The bottom line is that in most relationships, assuming we feel loved and respected by the other person, most of us are willing to make changes if they are couched in the form of a request rather than a demand. Such requests and subsequent changes can alleviate many of the irritating behaviors that stimulate anger.

In my opinion, processing distorted anger is much easier than processing definitive anger. Finding constructive rather than destructive methods of processing both is our objective.

HANDLING "BAD" ANGER

1. Share information. Tell the other person about your concern and ask to talk about it. Be sure to focus on the situation that sparked your emotion, rather than on the person.

2. Gather information. What are the facts?

3. Negotiate understanding. Express your struggles; then listen to the other person's response. Be honest.

4. Request change. As long as you neither demand nor manipulate for a change, this can have a positive outcome.

Anger repressed can
poison a relationship as surely
as the cruelest words.

DR. JOYCE BROTHERS

CHAPTER 6

EXPLOSIONS AND IMPLOSIONS

THE FLAME SHOT upward, fueled by a break in a city gas line. The line had ruptured when a private contractor, clearing land, clipped a gas pipe. At first just the pressurized gas poured out, hissing loudly. But within thirty minutes, a random spark had ignited the natural gas, which flamed skyward.

Within minutes the fiery plume was almost five stories high, and only a few yards away from Chicago public housing that lodged senior citizens. Fortunately, police and others evacuated the residents from the building. But when the gas company finally stopped the fuel feeding the line, scores of people had been displaced, their housing gutted or scorched.

Two months later, another explosion would displace Chicago residents. This time, though, the explosion was planned. A series of dynamite charges rigged by a demolition company popped in succession, and, one by one, four adjoining buildings at a different public housing project fell, crumbling to the ground and raising huge clouds of dust.

But this "explosion" was actually an *im*plosion, with building materials falling inward; the destruction had been planned for months, as part of an ongoing project to replace crime-infested, rundown housing with new, low-rise developments. In fact, former residents and other spectators watched a safe distance away, some applauding.

Which do you think was the more destructive event? Was it the gas-line explosion that charred the side of a building and left people without homes? Many would say yes. But in truth, both the gas explosion and the building implosion had equally destructive consequences. The imploding of the housing project destroyed more buildings and left many residents feeling a sense of loss for the home they had known for years. Likewise, implosive anger can be as damaging as explosive expressions of anger.

We have looked at constructive ways of responding to anger in the last three chapters, but let's be honest: Many of us have never learned to handle anger positively. We see that our responses to anger in the past have always made things worse. We find it hard even to believe that anger itself is not evil. We see the angry behavior of children, teenagers, and adults flashed before the world each day online and on TV, the crime and war and suffering that anger leaves in its path of destruction.

How then can we recognize—and control—harmful expressions of anger?

"I LOVE YOU TOO MUCH TO STAY AND LET YOU HURT ME": EXPLOSIVE ABUSE

Margaret was a screamer. When someone provoked her anger, whether child, husband, or employer, the person heard about it! Margaret prided herself on "speaking her mind." "At least people know where they stand with me," she often said. In truth, Margaret's anger was out of control. Beginning as a teenager, she had fallen into a pattern of verbally abusive behavior that had continued for twenty-five years.

Margaret justified her tirades until the day her daughter left her the following note. "Dear Mom, I won't be home tonight. I can't take your screaming anymore. I don't know what will happen to me, but at least I won't have to hear all the

> LET'S BE HONEST: MOST OF US HAVE NEVER LEARNED HOW TO HANDLE ANGER POSITIVELY.

nasty things you say to me when I don't do everything you want." She signed the note, *Lizzie*.

Margaret didn't scream when she read Lizzie's note. She called her pastor in tears. First she said only, "Lizzie has left; I don't know where she's gone. I'm so worried about her." Then she said the most hopeful thing she had said in years. "I drove her away. I know I drove her away. My screaming and yelling drove her away." Sobbing into the phone, she admitted for the first time that her angry tongue-lashings toward Lizzie were wrong. The pastor wisely guided Margaret to a Christian counselor, where she began the process of admitting, understanding, and changing her negative responses to anger.

Lizzie was located within forty-eight hours and later joined her mother in counseling. Today Lizzie, now a grown woman, has a good relationship with her mother. Margaret says that the day she got her daughter's note was the worst and best day of her life.

On the other hand, Paul's abuse tended toward the nonverbal. Whenever he was angry with someone, he would throw things, break things, and make rude gestures in traffic. Paul had gone so far as to hurl soft-drink bottles in family arguments.

Natalie had seen some of these characteristics in Paul before she married him, but he had never vented his anger toward her. But within six months after their wedding, he pushed her against the wall. She knew that his behavior was something she could not condone. She wrote him the following letter and mailed it to his office. "Dear Paul, Last night you did something I never thought you would do. In anger, you pushed me against the wall. I had seen you express anger while we were dating, but I never thought you would express it toward me. Now I know that I was wrong. I love you very much, and I don't believe that you really want to hurt me. But I cannot take that chance. I am writing you because I want you to know that if you ever touch me again in an angry way, I will leave and stay gone until I am assured by a counselor that it is safe to live with you. I love you. Nat."

The evening after Paul received the letter he apologized to Natalie and assured her that it would never happen again. Six months later, however, in a fit of anger, he grabbed her by the shoulders and shook her. Natalie didn't say a word, but the next day when he came home, Paul found the following note: "I love you too much to stay and let you hurt me and destroy your self-esteem. I know you cannot be happy about what happened last night. I will not return until your counselor assures me that you have learned to handle your anger in a more responsible manner. Love, Natalie."

Her decisive response motivated Paul to call his pastor and then a counselor. He knew that he was in danger of losing his wife. He also knew that he had to learn to control his anger. After three months of individual counseling and three months of marital counseling, Natalie and Paul were reunited. Years later, they are still together. Paul succeeded, with help, in breaking his pattern of abuse.

THE DESTROYER OF RELATIONSHIPS

Both Margaret and Paul fell into abusive patterns of expressing anger. Such behaviors form over a period of years and typically do not change unless someone important to the individual pressures the person to get help. It is the threat of losing a significant relationship that often motivates the abuser to get help. Help is readily available, and destructive, abusive patterns can be changed. But such patterns will not simply go away with time. Family members and friends must learn to hold the explosive person accountable for his or her destructive response to anger.

Explosive, angry behavior is never constructive. It not only hurts the person at whom it is directed, it destroys the self-esteem of the person who is out of control. No one can feel good about themselves when they think about what they have done. In the heat of such angry explosions, people say and do things they later regret. Undisciplined anger that expresses itself in verbal and physical explosions will ultimately destroy relationships. The person on the receiving end loses respect for the person who is out of control and will eventually just avoid them.

Some years ago it was popular in certain psychological circles to believe that releasing anger by aggressive behavior could be a positive way of processing anger if the aggression was not toward a person. Thus, angry people were encouraged to beat pillows, punching bags, and dolls or to take their aggression out on a golf ball. However, almost all research now indicates that the venting of angry feelings with such aggressive behaviors does not drain a person's anger but actually makes the person more likely to be explosive in the future.[1] Explosion, whether verbal or physical, is not an acceptable way of handling one's anger.

THE BOMBS OF IMPLOSION

In destroying any building through implosion, the demolition crew places the destructive power within the building rather than outside, keeping all the rubble and glass inside. This is a graphic picture of what happens to the person who chooses to hold anger inside. One's life literally crumbles around internalized anger. Whereas explosive anger is readily observed by the person's scream-ing, swearing, condemning, criticizing, and other words or acts of rage, implosive anger is not as easily recognized by others because it is, by definition, held inside.

Some Christians who would deplore explosive expressions of anger fail to reckon with the reality that implosive anger is fully as destructive in the long run. Whereas explosive anger begins with rage and may quickly turn to violence, implosive anger begins with silence and withdrawal but in time leads to resentment, bitterness, and eventually hatred. Implosive anger is typically characterized by three elements: *denial, withdrawal,* and *brooding.* Let's look at each of these.

Those who handle their anger "implosively" often begin by deny-ing that they are angry at all. This response to anger is especially tempting to Christians who have been taught that anger itself is sinful. Thus, one often hears individuals say one of the following:

- "I'm not angry, but I am very frustrated."
- "I'm not angry; I'm just upset."
- "I'm not angry, but I am disappointed."
- "I'm not angry; I just don't like it when people do me wrong."

In almost all these cases, however, their condition is the same: The people are experiencing anger.

Beverly illustrates this clearly. Sitting in my office on an October

ONE'S LIFE LITERALLY CRUMBLES AROUND INTERNALIZED ANGER.

morning, she said to me, "I know that Christians are not supposed to get angry, and I don't think I am, but I'm so upset at what has happened that I don't know what to do. My brother talked my parents into selling their house and giving him the money to start a business. He moved them into a small apartment, promised to pay their monthly rent as long as they lived, and said that if they ever needed to go to a retirement center, by then he would be able to afford it. He did all of this without discussing the matter with me. I know my brother. His business ideas are always wild. Within two years, he will lose all the money, and my parents will be on welfare.

"When I found out what had happened, I called him and he matter-of-factly told me about the whole process. He said he knew that I would not be upset because we both had talked earlier that they needed to be in a smaller place. I told him that I understood and I was sure it would work out. But the more I think about it, the more upset I get."

Beverly is obviously experiencing intense anger. Because she believes anger to be "unchristian," she doesn't want to call it anger, so she uses the word *upset*. However, the real denial was in her conversation with her brother. She gave him the impression that his actions were acceptable, whereas in reality she found them to be unacceptable. He doesn't know that she is angry; but, in fact, she is seething inside with anger. If she doesn't change her approach, the bombs of implosion will become deeply rooted inside of her and in due time her life will collapse. (See the likely results of implosive anger in next section.)

Denying anger does not make it go away. Internalized anger, whether admitted or not, will have its destructive effect upon the body and psyche of the angry individual. The anger will grow until denial is no longer possible.

But even more than denial, *withdrawal* is the central strategy of the people who struggle with implosive anger. While admitting anger to themselves and others, they withdraw from the person or situation that stirred up the anger. The idea is not denial—but distance. *If I can stay away from the person or at least not talk to him when I am with him, perhaps my anger will diminish with time*, the angry individual reassures herself. If the offending person notices the silent withdrawal and asks, "Is something wrong?" the withdrawer will respond, "No. What makes you think something's wrong?" If the person pursues the issue by saying, "Well, you've been quieter than usual. You haven't asked me about my day and you haven't said anything about yours," the withdrawer may respond, "I'm just tired. I had a hard day," as she walks out of the room.

HOW IMPLOSION DESTROYS

This "silent treatment," the withdrawal and avoidance, may last for a day or for years. The longer it continues, the more certain it is that resentment and bitterness will grow and fester.

Often this internalized anger will express itself in what the psychologists call *passive-aggressive behavior*. The person is passive on the outside, trying to give the appearance that nothing is bothering him, but eventually the anger emerges in other ways, such as failure to comply with a request the other person makes.

Andy, for example, was exhibiting passive-aggressive behavior toward his wife, Rachel. He was angry with Rachel because she expressed no interest in sexual intimacy. Though Andy refused to discuss the matter openly with Rachel, when she asked him to help with the kids' baths, he simply continued checking his emails, not even acknowledging her request. When she asked him to please wash some windows on Saturday, he planned an outing with his son. Most of the time Andy was not even fully conscious of what he was doing in his anger, but he was still getting back at her.

And what about Rachel? Her lack of interest in sexual intimacy also could have been a passive-aggressive act. She might have been storing her own anger toward Andy because he had failed to spend quality time with her. She would not discuss the issue that sparked her anger, but her anger had gone underground—but still showed itself in her behavior.

And so the passive-aggressive pattern begins a vicious cycle. Unless this destructive cycle is broken, it is only a matter of time until their marriage implodes.

The person dealing with internal anger may also *redirect* that anger. The individual redirects his or her angry feelings away from the person or situation that sparked the anger and toward another person or object. We are all familiar with the man who is angry with his boss but fears confronting the boss and chooses rather to come home, kick the cat, curse the children, and be verbally rude to his wife. This misplaced anger simply arouses more anger in the people who are abused and does nothing to deal with the situation that provoked the original anger.

This suppression of anger, holding anger inside, will eventually lead to physiological and psychological stress. There is a growing body of research that shows a positive correlation between suppressed anger and hypertension, colitis, migraine headaches, and heart disease.[2] However, the more pronounced results of suppressing anger are found in its impact upon one's psychological or emotional health. Internalized anger eventually leads to resentment, bitterness, and often hatred. All of these are explicitly condemned in Scripture and are viewed as sinful responses to anger.

A third characteristic of implosive anger is *brooding* over the events that stimulated the anger. In the person's mind, the initial scene of wrongdoing is played over and over like a videotape. He sees the other person's facial expression; he hears the person's words; he senses his spirit; he relives the events that stimulated the angry emotions. He replays the psychological audiotapes of his own analysis of the situation.

How could he be so ungrateful? Look at the number of years I've put into the company. He's only been here five years. He has no idea what's going on. If he knew how important I am to the company, he wouldn't treat me this way. I feel like resigning and letting him suffer. Or I feel like appealing to the board and getting him fired.

On and on the tapes play as one wallows in his or her anger. The difficulty is that the tapes play only in the person's head. The anger is never processed with the person involved or with a counselor or trusted friend. The anger is developing into resentment and bitterness. If the process is not interrupted, the person will eventually experience an implosion in the form of an emotional breakdown, depression, or in some cases, suicide.

However, for a growing number of these people who are internalizing anger, the end result will be not an implosion but an *ex*plosion. In their desperate emotional state, they will commit some act of violence toward the person who wronged them. This is seen over and over again on the nightly news when the employee who was fired nine months ago walks in and shoots the supervisor who fired him. At the age of fifteen the abused child murders her parents. The mousy husband turns on his wife and destroys her life. Neighbors are always shocked by such events, saying to the reporter, "He seemed like such a nice man. I can't believe that he would do such a thing." What the neighbor could not observe was the internalized anger that had been fed by brooding over a long period of time.

It should be obvious that implosive anger is fully as destructive as explosive anger. That is why the Scriptures always warn against internalizing anger. The apostle Paul admonished, "'In your anger do not sin': Do not let the sun go down while you are still angry, and do not give the devil a foothold" (Ephesians 4:26–27 NIV).

Clearly, Paul instructed that we are to process anger quickly, not allowing it to linger inside beyond sunset. I suppose that if we got angry after dark, he would give us till midnight, but the principle is that anger is not to be held inside; in fact, to do so is to give the Devil a foothold. That is, we are cooperating with Satan and setting ourselves up to sin even further. The apostle further challenged us to rid ourselves of anger. (See Ephesians 4:31; Colossians 3:8.) This is not an indication that anger itself is a sin; it is an indication that to allow anger to live inside is sinful.

Solomon warned that "anger resides in the lap of fools" (Ecclesiastes 7:9 NIV). The key word is *resides*; the fool lets the anger abide in him. The implication is that those who are wise will see that anger is quickly removed. Anger was designed to be a visitor, never a resident, in the human heart.

All of us experience anger for the reasons noted in earlier chapters. But holding anger inside by denying, withdrawing, and brooding is not the Christian response to anger. In fact, to do so is to violate the clear teachings of Scripture. Bitterness is the result of stored anger, and the Bible warns us against bitterness. (For example, see Acts 8:23; Romans 3:14; Hebrews 12:15.)

WATCH OUT FOR HATE

In the course of counseling through the years, I have heard teenagers say, "I hate my father." Almost always, such a statement is tied to a series of perceived wrongs committed by the father. The teenager has internalized the hurt and anger and has developed resentment, bitterness, and now hatred toward the father. I have also heard more than one wife say, "I hate my husband," and I've heard husbands express the same about their wives. Without exception, hatred does not develop overnight. Hatred is the result of internalized anger that remains planted in the heart of the individual.

Eventually the emotions of hurt from the internalized anger can harden into bitterness and even hatred. Almost always, those who hate wish ill upon the person at whom they are angry. Sometimes they end up perpetrating this ill themselves (as we noted in the examples above). The internalized anger erupts for all the world to observe.

When someone wreaks evil upon the individual who wronged them, he has usurped the prerogative of God. The Scriptures say, "Vengeance is mine; I will repay, saith the Lord" (Romans 12:19 KJV). When we seek to impose judgment upon those who have wronged us, we will inevitably make things worse.

HOW TO DEFUSE IMPLOSIVE ANGER

What positive steps can one take to defuse implosive anger? First, admit the tendency to yourself: "It's true; I hold my anger inside. I find it very difficult to share with others that I am feeling angry. I know I am hurting myself by doing this." These are the statements that lead to help. Second, reveal your problem to a trusted friend or family member. Telling someone else and asking for their advice may help you decide whether you should confront the person or persons with whom you are angry. Perhaps you will choose to "let the offense go," but at least this will be a conscious choice, and you can release your anger. If the person to whom you disclose your anger is unable to give you the help you need, then look for a pastor or counselor who can. Don't continue the destructive response of internalizing anger.

Perhaps you know a friend who seems to be harboring anger inside. Why not take the risk of helping him or her? You might begin, "I could be wrong, but I genuinely care about you, and that is why I am asking this question. Could it be that you are angry with someone and are holding it all inside? If I'm wrong, just tell me. But if it's true, I would like to help you process it. I know it isn't good to hold anger inside. Would you like to talk about it?"

Yes, you are running a risk by asking such questions. The person may tell you it is none of your business. On the other hand, your friend may open up, and your probing will be the first step in bringing his problem to the surface. If you are not able to help him further, then point the person to someone who can. A true friend does not sit silently and watch the self-destruction of a neighbor.

The clear challenge of Scripture is that we learn to process anger in a positive, loving manner rather than by explosion or implosion. The practice of explosive anger and implosive anger is not only highly destructive to the individual who is so handling anger but to everyone involved, including the community at large. Neither of these responses to anger can be accepted as appropriate in the life of a Christian. If you recognize either of these patterns in your own response to anger, I urge you to talk with a pastor, a counselor, or a friend; share with someone your struggle with these destructive patterns. You cannot reach your potential for God and good in the world if you continue to respond to your anger either by explosion or implosion.

That brings us to the next issue in handling our anger: What about the person who has been wronged for a lifetime and has stored the anger inside and has become an angry, resentful person? In the next chapter we address that question.

ARE YOU IN DANGER OF "IMPLODING"?

Definition: "Implosive" anger is internalized anger that is never expressed.

Sparked by: Fear of confrontation; belief that feeling or expressing anger is wrong.

How to recognize: Person denies that he or she is angry; responds by withdrawing; says things like, "I'm not angry, but I'm disappointed."

Results: Physiological and psychological stress; "passive-aggressive" behavior; can lead to resentment, bitterness, and even hatred and violence.

How much more grievous
are the consequences of anger
than the causes of it.

MARCUS AURELIUS

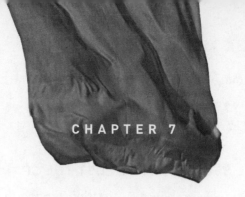

CHAPTER 7

THE ANGER THAT LASTS FOR YEARS

Mike was a mild-mannered, extremely successful physician. Yet his wife, Julie, had a major complaint. For the last year, he had been snapping at her and their boys for "every little thing," she said.

"I'm tired of it," she told me. "I don't know what is going on inside of him, but I know that it's not good for me and the boys to continue to hear his complaints. Nothing we do pleases him."

She explained that the early years of their marriage were great; Mike was very loving and caring. He seldom made a critical remark. But about two years ago he began to change, and Julie reported, "It's gotten worse over the last year." I asked what might have happened two years ago to affect Mike.

"Nothing I can think of," Julie replied. "His mother did die about that time, but she had been in a nursing home for four years and for the last year hardly knew who Mike was, so I don't think her death would have anything to do with this."

"HE SEEMS TO HAVE LOST THE SPARK"

"Is there anything else about your relationship that bothers you?" I asked.

"Mike seems to have lost his enthusiasm for life," she said. "He used to be so excited about his work and the family. He was always planning things for us to do. He rarely does that anymore. He seems to have lost the spark that used to be there."

At the conclusion of our session, I recommended that Mike come alone for the next session, and after that I'd like to see both of them together. Julie agreed.

Two weeks later when Mike and I got together, I briefly described Julie's visit and my desire to see him privately to get his perception of what was going on. "Then, if both of you are willing, I'd like to see the two of you together."

"Fine," Mike said. "I know that we've got some problems, and we need to deal with them."

"As you look at the earlier years of your marriage to Julie, how would you characterize those years?" I inquired.

"We had a good marriage. We did lots of things together. We enjoyed being with each other; we had lots of fun. When our boys were born, even though they required a lot of time, we still made time for each other. I think we had a good marriage. In fact, I think we still have a good marriage, but things have been a little rocky for the last year or so."

MIKE'S STORY

"From your perspective, what has made the marriage rocky over the last year or so?" I inquired.

"Well, I think I've been under a lot of stress at work," Mike said. "And I think the kids have become more demanding for Julie. She seems to stay tired all the time. I guess we're both under a lot of stress." Mike went on to describe his struggles with irritability and a lack of interest in things that used to engage him.

"In fact, I seem to have lost my bounce," he said. "I'm not very excited about my work or anything else. Frankly, this bothers me more than anything."

"How long have you been feeling this way?" I asked.

"A year or so, I guess. It just seems to have gotten worse within the last two months."

I asked Mike some questions about his childhood and learned he had a younger brother and a half-sister. "My dad left my mom when I was young. He remarried and had a daughter in that marriage. She's ten years younger than I, but actually I'm closer to her than I am my brother." His brother and he "did not get along very well," Mike explained. Then he added, "With Dad being gone, we both wanted to be the man of the house. It seems like we were always fighting about something. After I went to college and he went into the military, we didn't keep in touch very much."

His father was an alcoholic, he said. "When he was still at home, he was okay when he wasn't drunk, but when he got drunk, he was violent. I don't have good memories of my childhood. After Dad left, we didn't see him for about five years. But when I started college, he said he wanted to help me, which he did. After that, we saw each other once in a while, but we've never had a really close relationship."

"And what about your relationship with your mother?"

"Mom had her own problems," he said. "Maybe that's what drove Dad to drink; I don't know. She was very critical, not a warm person. After Dad left, she worked hard to make sure we had food and a place to live. I respect her for that, but she was hard on me and my brother. I was actually glad when it came time to go to college."

Unlike his father, Mike's mother did not remarry. She'd died about two years earlier, Mike said. In her later years she had developed Alzheimer's, and during the final three years before she died, her health steadily declined and she didn't always know her son when he visited.

"Do you think you have had a lot of resentment toward your mother and father over the years?" I asked.

"I don't know if it's resentment," he said. "I think I felt sorry for them through the years. Both of them had a rather empty life."

Mike revealed that in college he had fathered a child out of wedlock. The baby was put up for adoption. "Julie knows about this, but we have never told the kids. I don't think they need to know."

I could tell that Mike was being very vulnerable with me. I could also tell that he was beginning to feel uncomfortable. I changed the subject. "When you're driving a car and you're stopped at a traffic light, when the light turns green and the person in front of you doesn't move immediately, do you honk the horn?"

"I'm guilty," he replied. "I'm usually calm but when I get behind the wheel, I guess all my hostility comes out. You know, people do stupid things, so I yell at them if I'm by myself. If Julie and the kids are in the car, I try to keep it under control. But I've always been a horn blower!"

We laughed together. But then I continued: "I want to give you some food for thought. My guess is that you are a very angry man; that you have stored inside lots of anger over a long period of time."

Mike was silent for a moment, then said, "I never thought of myself as an angry person. In fact, I've always prided myself on handling my anger. I'm not the explosive type. I learned early on that it doesn't pay to fight. No, I don't see myself as an angry person."

"You may be right. We'll explore that further next time."

MIKE DIGS INTO HIS PAST

Before Mike left, I gave him some homework. "I want to ask that you get alone with pencil and paper. And I want you to think through your life, answering two questions: Who are the people who have done me wrong, and what have they done? You may want to make two columns on your paper, one entitled 'People' and the other 'Ways they have wronged me.' Begin with your earliest memory; focus on your childhood, your relationships with your mother, father, and brother. If all of them wronged you at one time or another, which would be pretty normal, list their names and list the ways in which they wronged you. Be specific when you have specific memories. For example, if your brother hit you over the head with a ball bat, put it down.

"Once you have finished with your family, take a look at your school career; go back as early as you can remember. Did a teacher or student wrong you? If so, put the person's name and what he or she did. Then look at other relationships that you may have had during childhood, relationships at church, in the neighborhood, during the teenage years, dating relationships. List everything that comes to mind. Then move to the college years. Think in terms of professors, fellow students, girlfriends, or others. Then go through your medical school experience, your residency, and all of your vocational settings up until the present. Then look at your relationship with Julie and the children. Begin with your dating relationship and move through your marriage.

"Think about your relationships with your extended family, business associates, and others. Try to be as comprehensive as you can. You can see why I said that this may take some time. I think it will be very helpful, so I want to ask you to give it your best efforts."

I sensed that Mike didn't know exactly where we were going with all of this, but he was intrigued with the idea and readily agreed. "I would also like to suggest that the two of us meet one more time before we invite Julie to join us."

"Fine," he said. "I'll tell Julie."

Two weeks later, Mike returned to my office with a yellow legal pad with three pages of names and events where he had been wronged throughout his life. "This assignment was very revealing," he said. "I've never thought about this before, and I never anticipated that I would come up with all of this. But once I started, my memory kicked in and it flowed faster than I could write. Actually, it was a very painful experience. I've never spent this much time thinking about my past. I've always been busy accomplishing my goals. My philosophy has been 'You can't change the past, so why bother with it?'"

"There's some truth to that philosophy, but there are two other realities," I said. "One is that we can learn from the past, and the other is that the past often affects our present behavior."

I took Mike's list, read his father's name first, and silently read the statements describing the wrongs that his father had done. Then I looked at Mike and asked, "Did you ever share these things with your father?"

"No," he said. "I learned early that you don't talk with my father, especially if you disagree with him."

I then read what he had written beside his mother's name and asked, "Did you ever share any of these things with your mother?"

"No, I didn't want to hurt Mom. She'd been through enough. I just tried to keep peace with her." I glanced down, reading his brother's name and the list beside his name. "Did you share any of these with your brother?" I asked.

"Well, when we were both at home, yes. Actually we fought about most of those things."

I continued down the list one by one, reading the names and events of people who had wronged Mike

> **"I'VE NEVER SPENT THIS MUCH TIME THINKING ABOUT MY PAST."
> —MIKE**

through the years. There were thirty-four names and numerous events. In only two cases had Mike processed his anger in a positive way. In the other thirty-two cases, Mike had simply tried to forget and move on.

THE HEAVINESS OF INJUSTICE

"Do you understand now why I guessed in our last session that you had a lot of anger stored inside?" I said.

"I think you were right, but how did you know?"

"Because you exhibited two common traits of stored anger," I continued. "One is to use your words—you 'complained a lot' about Julie and the children's behavior. To use Julie's words, you 'snapped at [her]' and the children. The other is your lethargic behavior over the past several months. To use your words, you've 'lost your bounce.' To use Julie's words, you 'seem to have lost the spark that used to be there.' I want to share with you why I believe this has happened.

"Throughout your lifetime, you have suffered some rather severe injustices. Understand, I'm not suggesting that all the people who have wronged you are bad people. What I'm observing is that a number of people in your life have done things that have deeply hurt you. Whenever we are wronged, anger is the natural emotion that arises within. The healthy way of handling that anger is to lovingly confront the person who has wronged us and work through it, seeking a resolution. Often, however, because of various circumstances, we are not able to do that. Children, for example, seldom process their anger toward parents—normally out of fear that the parents will not understand or that it will make things even worse. Thus, your response of not confronting your parents with your anger is very normal for children and teenagers.

"With your younger brother, you did process your anger somewhat by verbally arguing with each other and sometimes physically fighting each other. Neither of these led to a resolution of the issues that stimulated the anger. In most of the other situations that you have described, your response was to try to forget about the wrong that had been inflicted and to go on with your life. However, anger is not resolved that easily. In fact, wrongs are not forgotten unless they are processed. The fact that you can remember these several years after they happened indicates that you have not really forgotten them."

Mike was listening quietly, nodding his head at key points. I continued.

"Whenever we have experienced a series of wrongs over a long period of time, our emotional ability to absorb these wrongs is stretched beyond capacity. One of two things begins to happen.

We begin to express this anger not toward the people who perpetrated it through the years but toward other people in our present setting—in your case, toward Julie and the children. So you began to verbalize your anger by making critical remarks toward them. That is clearly a different approach from the one you have made through the years. The second way your anger is evidenced is by the beginning stages of depression.

"The purpose of our anger is to motivate us to take constructive action with the person who has wronged us, but if we fail to do this, unresolved anger becomes a dark cloud over our lives. We have been wronged, wronged, wronged—wronged throughout our lives by numerous people in numerous ways. The heaviness of all that injustice begins to settle upon our emotions. And we find ourselves becoming lethargic toward life, no longer interested in the things that used to stimulate our interest. If positive steps are not taken, the person goes on to become more and more explosive and/or more and more depressed."

"It all makes a lot of sense," Mike said. "But why did all of this just start happening only recently?"

"I think it was triggered by your mother's death," I responded. "Even though she had been sick and in the nursing home for the last three years of her life, I think her death touched the deep unresolved emotions that were inside and brought all this to the surface again. Before that time, the unresolved anger was covered by layers of activity that kept the conscious mind occupied on reaching worthwhile goals."

"Like a latent infection," Mike interjected, "waiting for a stimulant."

"Exactly."

"That makes a lot of sense," Mike said. "But what am I gonna do about it? I can't go back and talk to all these people. My mother's dead; my father would never understand. Some of the other people are also dead, and others, I have no idea where they live."

"That's true," I said, "so I'm going to make another suggestion. What I'm going to suggest will not rebuild relationships with any of these people. In fact, some of the people you no longer have a relationship with anyway. But what I'm going to suggest will process your anger in a positive way and allow you to change the two negative behaviors you are now experiencing."

I knew that Mike was a strong Christian and that he would understand the biblical foundation for what I was about to suggest. "I want to begin by reminding you about two basic fundamental characteristics of God. God is loving and God is just. God cares about the well-being of His creatures, but God is also just and ultimately will bring all men to justice. That's what the cross is all about—Christ took the full penalty of our sins. And for those who will accept that, God can forgive and still be just.[1]

"There's one other biblical concept. The Scriptures say that 'Vengeance is mine; I will repay, saith the Lord.'[2] It is never our job to vindicate ourselves by making people pay for the wrongs they've done toward us. They will either confess those wrongs to God and experience His forgiveness based upon what Christ has done for them, or they will face God with those sins, and He will be the ultimate and final judge."

RELEASING THE WRONG TO GOD

"Now here is what I want to suggest," I said, looking directly at Mike. "As soon as possible, I want you to take this legal pad and get alone with God. I want you to read each name and each offense to God; read it aloud. Then say to God, 'You know what my father did—this and this and this and this. And You know how wrong it was for a father to do these things to a child, and You know how much they hurt me. They've been inside all these years. But today, I want to release my father and all of these wrongs to You. You are a just God, and You are a loving God. You know everything about my father. I don't know what motivated him to do these things. You know his motives as well as his actions. And so I want to put him into Your hands and let You take care of him.

"'Do whatever You wish, whatever is good, whatever is loving. I put him into Your hands, and I release all of these wrongs to You, knowing that if he confesses them, You will forgive him. If not, You will deal with him on these matters. But I release them and give them to You today.'

"I want you to go through your whole list, everyone's name and everyone's actions and release them to God one by one, wrong by wrong," I told Mike. "Release them to God. Once you've done that, I want you to thank God that all of these things are now released to Him. I want you to ask God to fill your life with His Holy Spirit and give you the power to be the man He wants you to be in the future. And also ask Him for the ability to process future anger experiences when they occur. People will continue to do you wrong. Even Julie will do you wrong, and your children may do you wrong. But we are going to talk about how to process that anger in a positive way, and that's what I want you to learn.

"So you are going to ask God to teach you how to process your anger. Then as a symbol that you have released all these things to God and they are no longer in your life but in His hands, I want you either to burn or tear up and destroy these lists."

Two weeks later, Mike and Julie returned. Mike had shared with her what he had done. "It's been a good two weeks," Julie said. "This is one of the greatest things that has ever happened in our lives. I feel like I've got a new husband."

"It's been a good two weeks," Mike said. "The process of sharing those things with Julie was hard; sharing them with God was easier. But I feel like a load has been lifted."

"He hasn't been critical a single time this week," Julie said.

"Well, the anger is gone," Mike replied. "There's no need to be critical, and I'm beginning to feel excited about life again."

The rest of the session was spent helping Mike and Julie establish new guidelines for handling their anger in the future. Those guidelines are found in chapter 3. We had two more sessions dealing with other minor issues in their relationship. Mike and Julie had passed a significant milestone in their marriage, one that has greatly enhanced their marital intimacy and has enabled them to help many other couples over the past ten years.

ANGER AND DEPRESSION

After thirty-five years of counseling, I am convinced there are thousands of Mikes in the world, many of them extremely successful in their vocation and for many years untroubled by their hidden anger. But sooner or later, unprocessed anger will express itself either in violent behavior toward innocent people or in deep, unresolved depression, which keeps the individual from reaching his or her potential for God and good in the world. Please do not hear me saying that all depression is caused by unresolved anger. This is certainly not the case. But depression is sometimes the result of anger that is stored inside the individual over a long period of time.

When a person remains angry for the long term, he or she must process this anger to forestall those explosive or implosive responses. The process I have described in this chapter by sharing Mike's story would be helpful for anyone. Many people like Mike are totally unaware that past experiences are affecting their present behavior. Making a list of the wrongs perpetrated against us through the years is the first step in identifying unprocessed anger. Once the list is made, you may ask yourself, "How did I process my anger over this event?" If you find that it was not processed or was processed poorly, then it is never too late to deal with unresolved anger.

However, let me reiterate what I said to Mike: Processing our anger with God in this manner does not in and of itself rebuild relationships with the people who have wronged us. Rather it brings emotional and spiritual healing to us. Equally important, it makes our lives different in the future.

Whether one should go back and seek to deal personally with the individuals who wronged us is a decision that requires prayer and careful thought. There are numerous factors to consider, most of which we discussed in chapter 3 when we talked about processing anger with the person who wronged us. When this can be done, it brings the potential not only of personal healing but of healing the relationship. At the same time, it brings the potential for further rejection, hurt, and wrong. If the person is still alive and the relationship is still important, I recommend that one prayerfully consider this alternative. Usually such an attempt at reconciliation will be more productive if the individual has the assistance of a trusted pastor, counselor, or friend. (For a fuller exploration of the topic of reconciliation and apology, see my recent book *When Sorry*

Isn't Enough: Making Things Right with Those You Love, coauthored with Dr. Jennifer Thomas [Northfield].)

Such reconciliation always requires forgiveness—which brings us to the topic of our next chapter.

QUICK TAKES

SIX STEPS TOWARD DEALING WITH LONG-TERM ANGER

1. Make a list of (significant) wrongs done to you over the years.

2. Analyze how you responded to each event or person.

3. If the person is no longer living or available to reconcile, release your anger toward them to God.

4. For those still living, decide whether to seek reconciliation or to "let the offense go."

5. If you decide to proceed with reconciliation, bring a trusted third party, such as a pastor, to the meeting. This third party can act as a mediator or facilitator during the dispute and keep the dialogue on the main issue.

6. Seek forgiveness. Reconciliation almost always requires forgiveness, usually by you, but sometimes by the other party, whom you have perhaps unintentionally offended.

Forgiveness is not
a method to be learned as much
as a truth to be lived.

NANCY LEIGH DEMOSS

WHAT ABOUT FORGIVENESS?

Madison, a high school sophomore, had worked all summer getting ready for the cheerleader tryouts. When the tryouts were over, she felt good about her performance. A week later she discovered that she was not selected. She was crushed. Four days later she found out that Sophia, whom she thought to be her friend, had lied to the cheerleading coach, telling her that Madison was using drugs. Now Madison is livid with anger—valid anger, anger provoked by an injustice. She was sinned against by Sophia, whom she had trusted.

How should Madison—or any of us who feel sinned against by someone we trusted—respond? Where does forgiveness come in?

HOW GOD FORGIVES US

The Bible paints a picture of our wrongs against God, and how He chooses to respond. The prophet Isaiah thundered this message to ancient Israel: "It's your sins that have cut you off from God. Because of your sins, he has turned away and will not listen anymore" (Isaiah 59:2). We are never separated from God's love, but sin does separate us from His fellowship. The New Testament reminds us that "the wages of sin is death." Death is the ultimate picture of separation. Of course, this is not what God desires for His creatures; therefore, the writer quickly adds, "The free gift of God is eternal life through Christ Jesus our Lord" (Romans 6:23).

God desires fellowship with His creatures. That is what the cross of Christ is all about. God offers His forgiveness and the gift of eternal life.

In order to experience God's forgiveness, humans must respond to the call of God's Spirit with repentance and faith in Christ. (See Acts 2:37–39.)

The word *repent* means literally "to turn around." The message is clear: If we would receive God's forgiveness and enter into His eternal family, we must turn from our sin, acknowledge that Christ has paid the ultimate penalty for our sins, and accept God's forgiveness and gift of eternal life—all of this at the urging and guiding of the Holy Spirit.

The moment we do this, we experience the warm embrace of our heavenly Father. The distance is gone. To use John's words, we are now walking in the light, having fellowship with God. "And the blood of Jesus, his Son, cleanses us from all sin" (1 John 1:7).

Before we go further, let's clarify the meaning of the word *forgiveness*. The key ideas in the biblical languages are to cover, to take away, to pardon, and to be gracious to. The most common of these is the idea of taking away one's sins. For example, the psalmist says, "He has removed our sins as far from us as the east is from the west"

(Psalm 103:12). Thus, God's forgiveness is relieving the person from God's judgment—from the penalty due the sinner.

RECONCILIATION AND REPENTANCE

God's forgiveness toward us serves as a model of how we are to forgive others. The Scriptures say that we are to forgive each other, "just as God through Christ has forgiven you" (Ephesians 4:32). In this divine model, there are two essential elements—confession and repentance on the part of the sinner and forgiveness on the part of the one sinned against. In the Scriptures, these two are never separated.

For example, God's call to Israel was, "'This is what the LORD says: '. . . Come home to me again, for I am merciful. I will not be angry with you forever. Only acknowledge your guilt. Admit that you rebelled against the LORD your God. . . . Return home, you wayward children' says the LORD, 'for I am your master'" (Jeremiah 3:12–14). Never does God agree to reconcile while Israel continues in sin. There can be no reconciliation without repentance. In the New Testament, Jesus expressed the same reality when He said, "O Jerusalem, Jerusalem, the city that kills the prophets and stones God's messengers! How often I have wanted to gather your children together as a hen protects her chicks beneath her wings, but you wouldn't let me. And now, look, your house is abandoned and desolate" (Matthew 23:37–38). God cannot be reconciled to those who are unwilling to turn to Him.

There is no scriptural evidence that God ever forgave anyone who did not repent of sin and turn in faith to Him. Some would object by raising the following question: What about Jesus' prayer on the cross, "Father, forgive them, for they don't know what they are doing" (Luke 23:34)? Was that prayer not answered by the

Father? My response is, "Yes, but not immediately." Not only were they not immediately forgiven, but they continued in the dastardly act of crucifying the Son of God.

That they were not forgiven immediately is clear from Peter's sermon recorded in Acts 2, which took place on the day of Pentecost. Peter spoke to many of those who were responsible for the crucifixion of Christ when he said, "Fellow Israelites, listen to this: Jesus of Nazareth was a man accredited by God to you by miracles, wonders and signs, which God did among you through him, as you yourselves know. This man . . . you, with the help of wicked men, put . . . to death by nailing him to the cross. But God raised him from the dead. . . . With many other words he warned them; and he pleaded with them" (Acts 2:22–24, 40 NIV).

He was obviously preaching to some who actually participated in the crucifixion of Christ. More than three thousand responded to the truth and acknowledged Christ as Savior (verse 41). The rest of Acts records numerous others who responded to Christ. And in Acts 6:7 we read, "The number of believers greatly increased in Jerusalem, and many of the Jewish priests were converted, too." Apparently, it was after Pentecost when many of those who crucified Jesus came to acknowledge Him as the Messiah and experienced God's forgiveness. Jesus' prayer on the cross, "Father, forgive them, for they do not know what they are doing," is an indication of His willingness and deep desire that they experience the Father's forgiveness. It is this willingness to forgive that we must emulate. But those for whom He prayed did not experience the Father's forgiveness until they repented and placed their faith in Christ the Messiah.

REBUKING—AND REBUILDING TRUST

Let's go back to Madison, who felt betrayed by her friend. What should she do?

Let's look at the biblical paradigm laid out by Jesus in Luke 17. "If another believer sins, rebuke that person; then if there is repentance, forgive. Even if that person wrongs you seven times a day and each time turns again and asks forgiveness, you must forgive" (verses 3–4). Notice the progression of events. First, there is a sin committed—your brother, sister, or friend treats you unjustly. Immediately you experience valid righteous anger. Your first response is clear: You are to rebuke the person who sinned against you. As noted earlier, the word *rebuke* means to place a weight upon, to bring a matter to the attention of. In short, you confront the other person with his or her sin.

As we've discussed, it is usually best to give yourself time to cool down emotionally before you make this rebuke. But to think that you are going to be totally calm when you have been sinned against in such a radical way is to be unrealistic. However, you must be careful not to sin in your rebuke. You must treat the person as one for whom Christ died. You must exhibit Christian love so that your deepest desire is that the person will confess and repent of her wrong so that you may extend forgiveness.

YOU MUST BE CAREFUL NOT TO SIN IN YOUR REBUKE.

The next step is that the person who has sinned must repent; that is, she must confess the wrong committed and express a desire to turn from practicing that wrong in the future. If this is done, then Jesus said we are to forgive the person. We are to lift the penalty and receive the individual back into a restored relationship with us. And we begin the process of rebuilding trust. We refuse to allow someone's misdeed to keep us away from her, and we do not allow our feelings of hurt and disappointment to control our behavior toward her. We forgive her in the same manner that God has forgiven us and in the same manner that we hope she would forgive us if we sinned against her.

Forgiveness, however, does not remove all the effects of sin. When David sinned against Bathsheba and her husband, God fully forgave David when he confessed his sin. But the negative results of David's sin plagued him throughout the remainder of his life. The same is true of our sin. Let me illustrate. Let's say that I commit the sin of drunkenness, and in my drunken state I drive my car down the highway. A short time later, I veer off the road, run into a utility pole, and in so doing break my leg and extensively damage my car. I may confess my sin to God before I get out of the car and experience God's forgiveness. But my leg is still broken and my car is still twisted, even though I am forgiven by God. My wife shows up at the scene, and now I am faced with the reality that I have sinned against her. If I confess my wrong to her and if she chooses to forgive me, I now have the opportunity for rebuilding her trust in me. But she too will suffer; she too will be affected when our car insurance rate goes up because of my accident, and when my license is removed and she must drive me to work. I am forgiven by my wife and God, but I must continue to face the results of my wrong as the news spreads through the community.

No, *forgiveness does not remove all the results of sin.* I must be held accountable for my actions, and I must seek to learn through my failures.

A second reality of forgiveness is that *forgiveness does not remove all of my painful emotions.* My wife may well forgive me, but when she thinks about what I did, she may once again feel disappointment and anger toward me. Forgiveness is not a feeling; it is a commitment to accept the person in spite of what he or she has done. It is a decision not to demand justice but to show mercy; that is what the forgiving wife (or husband) must do. Nor does forgiveness mean that I will never think of the situation again. Because every event in life is recorded in the brain, there is every potential that the event will return to the conscious mind again and again.

If we have chosen to forgive, we take the memory to God along with the hurt feelings, acknowledge to Him what we are thinking and feeling, but thank Him that by His grace our sin has been forgiven. Then we ask Him for the power to do something kind and loving for that person today. We choose to focus on the future and not allow our minds to be obsessed with past failures that are now forgiven.

"BUT IF HE WILL NOT LISTEN . . ."

But what if the person does not repent? Am I still to forgive the person? The biblical answer is clear, and it is found in the teachings of Jesus. "If another believer sins against you, go privately and point out the offense. If the other person listens and confesses it, you have won that person back. But if you are unsuccessful, take one or two others with you and go back again, so that everything you say may be confirmed by two or three witnesses. If the person still refuses to listen, take your case to the church. Then if he or she won't accept the church's decision, treat that person as a pagan or a corrupt tax collector" (Matthew 18:15–17). The principles of church discipline delineated by Jesus apply fully as well in any close relationship we have (including non-Christians), and it answers the question as to what we do if the person does not repent after our loving confrontation. We broaden the circle of experience by inviting two trusted friends to join us in confronting the erring person once again. If there is still no repentance, then we treat the person as an unbeliever.

How do Christians treat unbelievers? We pray for them; we seek to be kind to them, but we do not treat them as though they were innocent, for they are not. Remember, all sin brings separation. The separation is not removed by our choosing to overlook the sin. Sin always creates barriers in human relationships, and the barriers only come down when there is genuine repentance and genuine forgiveness.

Consider a wife—we'll call her Angie—who discovers her husband, Tom, is having an affair. Angie confronts Tom with what she has discovered. He may have one of several responses. He may deny the allegations until he is convinced she has evidence. He may confess and promise her that he will sever the relationship with the young woman at work. He may tell her that he is in love with the young woman and that he wants a divorce so he can marry her. He may confess and actually break the relationship with the other person.

It is only the last of these options that will make forgiveness possible. If Angie is to forgive and Tom is to receive genuine forgiveness, he must begin with confession and repentance. Then, together, they can work on rebuilding their marital relationship.

SHOULD WE FORGIVE TO AVOID PERSONAL BITTERNESS?

Back to Madison. Should she forgive her friend simply for her own benefit—so that anger does not harden into bitterness against Sophia? I would certainly agree that Madison should release her anger before it turns to bitterness. But from a biblical perspective, forgiveness cannot be a one-way street. Forgiveness is a gift, one that cannot be opened until the sinner is willing to admit that "I need it and I want it."

There is no scriptural evidence that God ever forgives the unconfessing, unrepentant sinner. God is always willing to forgive, desirous of forgiving, but He cannot actually forgive until the sinner repents.

The same is true in human relationships. Christians with the aid of the Holy Spirit must always stand ready to forgive, willing and desirous of forgiving, extending forgiveness, but we cannot force forgiveness to someone who does not desire it.

What then should Christians do with their angry feelings and thoughts when the person who wronged them refuses to repent of the wrong committed? I believe that we are to lovingly confront the person as God confronts us. If the individual does not respond positively to our first confrontation, we should pray for him and make another attempt, perhaps inviting one or two others to go with us, thus broadening the circle of knowledge about the sin. If the person does not respond in due time to this confrontation, then the reality of the sin must be shared with the larger community, which typically involves the extended family and, in some cases, the church family.

If the person still does not repent of the wrong, then he or she is to be treated as a "pagan." This is the word Jesus used. The Matthew 18 passage primarily addresses relationships between Christian believers, but the principle applies to all who would let sin fracture a relationship. A pagan was an outsider, an unbeliever. Whether the offending person is an actual unbeliever or just an unrepentant sinner, we treat the individual the same, as one who has broken fellowship with us. To treat the person as a pagan means we do not regard him as a close friend. We should continue to pray for him, to be kind to him, to treat him with dignity and respect. Remember, here is a person for whom Christ died, a person with whom we would desire to be reconciled. But we cannot act as though the sin does not exist. The fact is the sin has created a barrier between the two of you, and the barrier will not dissolve with time alone.

I am often frustrated when I hear Christians admonish each other that they must forgive the offending party even if the person is unwilling to confess and repent of his sin. How many Christian wives have been put in an untenable position by pastors who encourage them to forgive husbands who are having affairs even though the husband refuses to repent? I understand the intention of the pastor's advice. He wants the wife to be free of the anger, bitterness, and perhaps hatred that has built up in her heart toward the husband and is destroying her own well-being. He desires to see her freed from all of that and walking in fellowship with God, not allowing her husband's sin to destroy her life. This intention is wholly admirable, but a nonbiblical forgiveness is not the answer.

TWO DECISIVE STEPS:
RELEASE TO GOD; CONFESS ANY PERSONAL SIN

I believe the answer lies in taking two decisive steps. *First, commit or release the person who has sinned against you to God*, letting God take care of that person rather than insisting that you pay him back for the wrongful action. The Scriptures teach that vengeance belongs to God, not to man. (See Romans 12:19.) The reason for this is that God alone knows everything about the other person, not only his actions but his motives. And God alone is judge. So the person who is eaten up with bitterness toward another who has treated him unfairly is to release that person to an all-knowing heavenly Father who is fully capable of doing what is just and right toward that person.

The apostle Paul demonstrated this when he said to young Timothy, "Alexander the coppersmith did me much harm, but the Lord will judge him for what he has done. Be careful of him, for he fought against everything we said" (2 Timothy 4:14–15). Not only had Paul not forgiven Alexander because Alexander had not repented, but Paul warned Timothy to be on his guard because Alexander may also treat him unjustly. Paul did not whitewash the matter by offering an easy forgiveness to Alexander. Instead, he did the responsible thing by turning Alexander over to God. After Paul made this decision, I don't think he lost any sleep over Alexander. His anger was processed by the conscious act of turning the offender over to a just and merciful God.

Peter indicated that Jesus Himself took a similar approach. Having discussed the sufferings of Christ, Peter said, "He did not retaliate when he was insulted, nor threaten revenge when he suffered. He left his case in the hands of God, who always judges fairly" (1 Peter 2:23).

ANGER WAS DESIGNED TO BE A VISITOR, NEVER A RESIDENT.

As a man, Jesus did not take the prerogative of taking revenge on those who had wronged Him; rather, He committed the whole situation to God, knowing that God would judge righteously. Often when we have been wronged, we think that if we don't press the issue and demand justice, then no one will. The fact is that God is in a far better position to be the judge than we. You can turn your erring friend and the wrong committed against you over to God, knowing that He will take the best possible action on your behalf. He is more concerned about righteousness than you are.

The second crucial step is for the person who has been sinned against to confess any of his own sin. Remember, anger itself is not sin, but often we allow anger to lead us to sinful behavior, such as an explosion or implosion (discussed in chapter 6). Thus angry employees returning to shoot it out with the supervisor are sinful; they are committing their own wrong and are compounding the problem. However, when we unleash verbal tirades against the person who has wronged us, or if we commit acts of physical violence, we also are sinful. And let's not forget implosive anger: Anger held inside often becomes bitterness and hatred, both of which are condemned in Scripture as sinful.

As noted in an earlier chapter, anger was designed to be a visitor, never a resident. The biblical challenge is that we are to rid ourselves "of anger, rage, malicious behavior, slander, and dirty language" (Colossians 3:8). When you or I become obsessed with our own hurt and anger, we are no longer focusing on God and are guilty of misguided passion. If ever there is a time when we need the help and guidance of God, it is when we have been wronged by a friend or family member.

At that point, prayer is vital. The following prayer may help you take these two steps toward alleviating your own inner turmoil.

Father, You know the pain, the hurt, the anger, the bitterness that I feel toward _____. You know what he (she) has done to me. You know that I have made every effort to seek reconciliation, but he is unwilling to deal with the wrong. You know his response to me and You know his continued lifestyle. I recognize that he is beyond my control. I cannot make him do what I wish he would do. So I want to commit _____ to You, knowing that You are a just and honest God, and that in the future, You will treat him justly. So I put _____ in Your hands and trust You to work in his life what is best.

I also want to confess that I have allowed his wrong to consume me. I have become obsessed with my anger, my hurt, my disappointment, my frustration. I've had a bitter spirit toward this person, sometimes toward You for allowing this to happen. I want to confess that this is wrong, and I want to thank You that Christ has paid my penalty. I want to accept Your forgiveness for my wrong attitudes.

I pray that Your Spirit will fill my heart and my mind, and help me to think Your thoughts and to do only those things that will be helpful in my situation. I don't want my life to be ruined because of what the other person has done to me, and I know that is not Your desire. Guide me today as I read Your Word, as I seek the right kind of Christian friends, as I look for Christian books that will help me, as I seek to put my life back in Your hands. I want to follow You. I want to accomplish Your purposes. Let this be a day of new beginnings for me. In the name of Christ, my Savior and Lord. Amen.

Such a prayer, prayed sincerely, will channel the Christian's energies in the right direction, namely, toward seeking God's fellowship and wisdom. If and when the other person confesses and repents of wrongdoing, we must stand ready to forgive and work at rebuilding the relationship.

In the meantime, we are walking in the light, having fellowship with God, knowing that God's purposes for our lives will not be thwarted because of what someone else has done. In fact, the Scriptures say that God will turn even the wrongs done to us into something positive. (See Romans 8:28–29.) Let me be clear in noting that such action does not restore the fellowship with the person who has wronged you, but it does liberate you to go on with your life and to use your time and energy in a more constructive way.

ASKING FORGIVENESS FOR *OUR* SINS

In this chapter, we have talked primarily about our responsibility to confront family members and friends who sin against us and to seek reconciliation. However, there is another word from Jesus. It has to do with our own sin. His instructions are clear. "So if you are presenting a sacrifice at the altar in the Temple and you suddenly remember that someone has something against you, leave your sacrifice there at the altar. Go and be reconciled to that person. Then come and offer your sacrifice to God" (Matthew 5:23–24).

When we sin against others, it is our responsibility to confess and repent of our own sins. We should take the initiative as soon as we realize that we have done or said something unfairly to another. Thus, it will be clear to the astute reader that whether I have sinned against someone else or someone has sinned against me, it is my responsibility to take the initiative to seek reconciliation. If I have sinned against someone, very likely the person is experiencing anger toward me. If the person has sinned against me, then I am the one experiencing anger. In God's plan, anger is designed to motivate us to take constructive action in seeking to right the wrong and restore the fellowship with the other person.

FORGIVING WHEN YOU'VE BEEN WRONGED

1. Rebuke the offending person—bring the offense to his or her attention. Do this only after you have calmed down emotionally.

2. Wait for the person to admit his wrongdoing and express a desire to turn from practicing that wrong in the future. When the individual does this, you should forgive him or her.

3. Even after the person repents, realize that there might be lasting scars from the event. You may still struggle with anger or disappointment, but remember that forgiveness entails a commitment to accept the person in spite of what he or she has done.

The greatest remedy for anger
is delay.

SENECA

CHAPTER 9

WHEN YOU ARE ANGRY AT YOUR SPOUSE

"I don't ever remember losing my temper until I got married."

Dan may have had a faulty memory about his years before marriage, but one thing he was certain of: Sarah provoked his anger. "When she says certain things or gives me 'that look,' I get furious."

Sarah would make sarcastic, rhetorical comments like, "Are you going to fix that broken chair, or do I have to ask my father to come over and do it?" "That look" to which Dan referred happened when Sarah set her head a certain way and stared at him. "That look," he said, "is worse than a thousand condemning words. What I see in her eyes is, 'I'm sorry I married you.'"

Dan was angry because Sarah struck at his self-esteem. Most of us want to be liked, accepted, and appreciated. When we're criticized we tend to respond defensively. Sarah may argue that she is criticizing Dan's behavior, not his person, but since our behavior is an extension of who we are, it is difficult for most of us, including Dan, to make the distinction. Something deep within Dan said, "It's not right for my wife to put me down."

The tone of Sarah's voice indicated that she too was angry. She has likely concluded that Dan is not doing his fair share around the house. The broken chair sits unfixed while he twiddles on his phone. She takes out the garbage while he obliviously watches TV. That is not exactly her idea of a loving husband.

All married couples experience anger. Experiencing anger is not wrong. The tragedy is that thousands of couples have never learned how to process anger productively. Thus, they explode in tirades that do nothing but make the situation worse, or they suffer in isolated silence as they withdraw from each other. Most of us can look at our own childhood and remember picnics that were spoiled not by the rain but by the parents' anger toward each other. How many birthdays have been ruined by the bickering of parents who have not learned to resolve their anger? How many holidays have become days of horror because of the reign of anger?

> "WHAT I SEE IN HER EYES IS, 'I'M SORRY I MARRIED YOU.'"

Sadly, most married adults have never learned how to handle anger properly. Marriage becomes a battlefield, each spouse accusing the other of firing the first shot. If the couple do not learn to properly handle their anger, they will never have a satisfying marriage. I say "never" because love and uncontrolled anger cannot coexist. Love seeks the well-being of the spouse, while uncontrolled anger seeks to hurt and destroy.

SIX KEYS TO ANGER MANAGEMENT

The good news is that couples can learn to handle anger responsibly. In fact, they must learn if they are to survive. I'm not suggesting that learning to handle anger is an easy process. I am suggesting that it is a necessary one, and any couple can be successful. Built upon the principles of anger management described in chapter 3, let me suggest a six-step strategy for handling anger in marriage.

First, *acknowledge the reality of anger.* In the course of marriage, each of us will experience anger from time to time. Some of this anger will be definitive, spurred by wrong action on the part of the spouse. Some of this anger also will be distorted, stimulated by a misunderstanding of what happened. We will each experience a fair share of both types of anger. This is a part of being human and living life with each other.

Remember, anger is not sinful; rather, it is evidence that we have a concern for fairness and justice. Thus, we do not need to condemn ourselves or each other for experiencing anger, nor do we need to deny that we are angry.

When we give each other the right to feel anger, we are giving each other the right to be human. This is the starting place in learning to process anger positively.

Second, *agree to acknowledge your anger to each other.* When you are angry with each other, give the other the benefit of knowing what you are feeling. Otherwise, the spouse must guess based on your behavior. Such "guessing games" are a waste of time and usually not very accurate. If you are angry toward your spouse, it's because he or she has done or said something that you deem inappropriate, or failed to do or say something that you expected. In your mind, he or she has done you wrong. Your partner has treated you unkindly, unfairly, or inappropriately. You do not view the behavior as loving. At that moment, the event—the inappropriate action of your spouse—has become a barrier between the two of you. Your spouse deserves to know this. He cannot work on a problem of which he is unaware.

We each deserve the benefit of knowing when our spouse is angry and what she is angry about. The couple who commit to give each other this information have taken a major step in resolving anger productively.

Third, *agree that verbal or physical explosions that attack the other person are not appropriate responses to anger.* Such unhealthy venting of anger is always destructive and should not be accepted as appropriate behavior. This does not mean that once your spouse and you make this agreement neither of you will ever "lose your cool" again; however, it does mean that when you do so, you're committed to acknowledging that the response was wrong. Explosive expressions of anger always makes things worse, and the debris from such explosions must be cleared before we can deal constructively with the event that stimulated the original anger.

One practical way to break this negative practice of explosion is to agree that whenever either of you begins to explode, the other will walk out of the room, and if you are followed, you will walk out of the house. If the spouse pursues you in the yard with yelling and screaming, you will run to a neighbor's house or around the block. If you both agree to this strategy, then each of you will know that when the other starts walking or running, it's time to stop and reflect on what is happening. The hope is that when you return from the walk or run, your spouse will have calmed down and will be able to say, "I'm sorry. My exploding at you was wrong. I guess I was so hurt and angry I lost control. I'm sorry. Please forgive me." You can then forgive your spouse for this momentary lapse, and you can pursue the issue that originally aroused his or her anger.

Fourth, *agree to seek an explanation before passing judgment.* If you are angry with your spouse, your first impression is that his behavior is wrong. But you should always take this as tentative until you hear his side. We often misinterpret the words and actions of our spouses. For instance, he forgot to bring the milk home even after he wrote himself a note. She interprets this as irresponsibility, and she experiences anger. But it may be: the store was out of milk; he took a colleague home from the office and didn't go by the store; or he knew she didn't need the milk for dinner and plans to get it when he picks up Lindsay from gymnastics. If she is committed to seeking an explanation, she will hold her judgment of irresponsibility as tentative until she hears his perspective.

Rob thought he heard his wife say on the telephone that he was "late and that she couldn't stand being late." He felt angry because he had made every effort to be there on time and was only two minutes late. When he sought an explanation, he found that she was actually talking about a friend's baby who arrived two weeks late. If actions and words are open to misunderstanding, motives are even more difficult. Since motives are internal, we can never know another person's motives unless he or she tells us. We often attribute motives to our spouse that are totally off base.

Jonathan was acting wisely when he said, "I may really be misreading this, and that's why I'm asking for an explanation. It appears to me that you charged $300 at Macy's. I thought we agreed that neither of us would spend over $100 without consulting the other until we get our debts under control." He was shocked by Bethany's response.

"Oh, darling, I can explain. Our section at work went in together and bought Betsy a retirement gift. They asked me to pick it up during my lunch hour since I was meeting Ginger at the mall. So I put the whole thing on Visa, but they each gave me $20. It's in my purse. I think I have $300. If so, my part is only the tax."

Jonathan's anger subsided as he counted the $300. Then he smiled as he remembered what his response would have been six months ago, before he and Bethany took a marriage enrichment class and learned how to process anger. He could visualize his face getting red and his voice exploding to Bethany about what she had done. "I really am making progress," he said aloud.

"What are you talking about?" Bethany asked.

"I was just thinking about how I would have responded before we took the marriage enrichment class." Jonathan was smiling now. "I would have been furious and would not have asked for an explanation. Then I would have felt stupid afterward when you told me what happened. I much prefer our new system." Jonathan and Bethany have learned the benefit of seeking an explanation before making final judgments.

Fifth, *agree to seek a resolution.* In the case of Jonathan and Bethany, Jonathan's anger was resolved once he received Bethany's explanation. Obviously not all anger resolution is that easy. Let's assume that Bethany had actually broken their commitment and had made a $300 purchase after agreeing that neither of them would purchase anything over $100 without discussing it with the other. Let's assume her explanation was, "But, honey, it was on sale. I saved $200, and we need it. I didn't think you would object."

"Well, I do object," Jonathan replies. "It would be nice to have it, but we don't really need it. We've gotten along quite well without it, and we can't afford to add $300 to our debt. We made an agreement, and you have broken the agreement. And I think that is wrong."

Bethany replies, "I'm surprised at your response. I really didn't think that you would object. I thought you wanted it as much as I did."

"I do want it, sweetheart. I would like to have it, but we cannot afford it. And we agreed to draw the line on purchases, and I think we must stick to our agreement."

"Well, if you insist. I can take it back," Bethany says. "I don't want to, but I will."

"It's not a matter of wanting," says Jonathan. His voice is firm but not loud. He is in control of his feelings and offers an explanation. "I would like to keep it, but the bottom line is we can't afford it now. I wish we could, but you know our situation as well as I do."

"Okay," says Bethany. "Then I'll take it back."

"Fine. You do know that I love you and someday we will buy it," adds Jonathan, putting his hand on her shoulder.

"I know you love me, and in retrospect it was a poor decision. I'm glad you are holding me to our agreement."

Some of you are asking, Is that not extremely idealistic? My response is, Not for couples who have learned how to process anger responsibly and who are committed to loving each other.

Sixth, *agree to affirm your love for each other.* After the anger is resolved, tell each other of your love. In doing so you are saying, "I am not going to allow this event to separate us." As a couple, you have heard each other out, the issue has been resolved, you have learned from the experience, and you move on together.

Where genuine wrong has been committed, where one has been

unkind, unloving, or unjust, resolution requires confession and repentance on the part of the one who committed the indiscretion and forgiveness on the part of the other. Anger subsides when this process has been completed. Anger has served its noble purpose of holding each of us accountable for our behavior.

In the case of distorted anger, where the anger is aroused by a perceived wrong that later turns out to be a misunderstanding, resolution comes by means of seeking an explanation and finding that one's original interpretation of events was wrong. The person who has not learned the difference between definitive anger and distorted anger will assume that his anger is always legitimate and the other person's actions always wrong. Such an assumption does not allow anger to be resolved and will, in fact, stimulate anger in the spouse who knows that your anger is distorted. Your rigid insistence on being right will stimulate anger in your spouse that also needs to be resolved.

One can easily understand how unresolved anger can snowball and become an ever-increasing problem as the marriage goes on. Few things are more important to a successful marriage than learning to resolve anger in a responsible manner.

I believe a genuine commitment to these six principles will get a couple on the pathway toward productive anger management. Marriages need not be destroyed by uncontrolled anger. The Christian must set the pace in learning how to handle anger responsibly. It is my sincere desire that this book will help thousands of couples come to grips with what has become a major problem in Christian marriages. If you are married, I urge you to mutually commit yourselves to these six principles and begin today to practice them.

"IS THIS A GOOD TIME TO TALK?"

In my efforts to help couples get started, I have often suggested the following exercise. On a three-by-five card, write the following words:

> I'm feeling angry right now, but don't worry. I'm not going to attack you. But I do need your help. Is this a good time to talk?

Put this card on the refrigerator door or some other easily accessible place. The next time you feel anger toward your spouse, run for the card. Holding it in your hand, read it to your spouse as calmly as you can. If it's not "a good time to talk," then set a time to talk. And at the appointed time, begin the process of seeking an explanation and resolution of the issue that stimulated your anger. In this brief written speech, you have acknowledged that you are experiencing anger, you have affirmed your commitment not to explode, and you have expressed your desire for an explanation and resolution through conversation.

When you sit down to discuss the issue, begin by saying, "I know that I could be misunderstanding this and that's why I wanted to talk with you. Let me tell you what I am feeling and why. Then if you can clarify the situation, please do so, because I need help in resolving this." Such a beginning creates a nonthreatening atmosphere in which to discuss the event that sparked your anger.

In every marriage, anger will make its occasional visit for reasons discussed throughout this book. I believe that anger is a friend, not an enemy. The Christian couple who understand the source of anger and the purpose of anger has also the aid of the Holy Spirit to practice this disciplined biblical approach to resolving anger in a constructive manner. This lesson is one of the most important you will ever learn and is an essential ingredient to a successful marriage.

DEALING WITH ANGER TOWARD YOUR SPOUSE

Here are six steps for dealing with anger you feel toward your spouse. Most of these six steps should be in place before the anger comes; that way, when it appears, an agreed-upon plan can help calm and direct the discussion.

1. Acknowledge the reality of anger. Whether your anger is legitimate definitive anger or distorted anger, do not condemn yourself for experiencing anger. Recognize and admit to it, remembering that the anger itself is not sinful.

2. Agree to acknowledge your anger to each other. Express clearly your feeling of anger when it arises; do not make your spouse guess based on your behavior. Both you and your spouse deserve to know when the other is angry and what he or she is angry about.

3. Agree that verbal or physical explosions against the other person are not appropriate responses to anger. Either kind of explosion will always make things worse.

4. Agree to seek an explanation before passing judgment. Remember that your first impression is only tentative; at times it will be faulty. It is easy to misinterpret the words and actions of one's spouse, so seek your mate's perspective. He or she may supply valuable missing information that could change your understanding of the issue.

5. Agree to seek a resolution. With more information from

your spouse and the fuller perspective, you are ready to find a solution satisfactory to both of you. Resolving the angry feelings may require that you seek the person's confession and repentance—if the wrongdoing is valid and definitive—or recognize your anger as invalid and perhaps selfish—if the anger is distorted. It may even require confession and asking of forgiveness on your part, if the wrongdoing is by you. Whatever the cause, work toward a reconciliation between the two of you.

6. Agree to affirm your love for each other. After the anger is resolved, verbally declare your love for each other.

These six principles for dealing with anger toward your spouse are so important that I have summarized them as a "Quick Take" (next page). Again, keep in mind that most of these six steps should be in place before anger appears, so that when it occurs, you have a plan to help direct the discussion. With these six "anger agreements" between husband and wife, you can have an effective strategy for resolving anger in marriage.

QUICK TAKES
ANGER AGREEMENTS IN MARRIAGE

1. Acknowledge the reality of your anger, remembering that anger itself is not sinful.

2. Agree to acknowledge anger to each other. Do not make your mate "guess" about how you're feeling.

3. Agree that verbal or physical explosions against the other person are not appropriate reactions to anger—they will always make things worse.

4. Agree to seek an explanation before jumping to conclusions. The person may supply valuable missing information that could change your understanding of the issue.

5. Agree to seek resolution and reconciliation. With more information from your spouse and the fuller perspective, you are ready to find a solution satisfactory to both of you.

6. Agree to affirm your love for each other. After the resolution is found, verbally declare your love for each other.

Do not teach your children
never to be angry; teach them how
to be angry and sin not.

LYMAN ABBOTT

CHAPTER 10

HELPING CHILDREN HANDLE ANGER

Michelle, a single mom, is trying to prepare Sunday lunch. Meanwhile, six-year-old Ella and eight-year-old Will are playing in the den. At least Michelle thought they were playing—but suddenly it sounds more like warfare than play. As Michelle walks into the den, she sees Will hit his sister across the back with a stuffed bear. Ella begins to cry.

"She stole my book," Will says.

"I did not!"

Michelle grabs Will by the arm, plants a solid blow to his backside, and says, "Go to your room and don't come out till I call you." Then she turns to Ella and says, "How many times have I told you not to mess with your brother's things?"

"I didn't," Ella protests. "I was just trying to get on the couch to watch TV and he hit me."

"I don't want to hear it," Michelle says. "I can't even get lunch ready without you two fighting. You go to your room, and I'll call you when lunch is ready."

"You always blame me!" Ella says as she runs to her room.

In the kitchen, Michelle hears Ella's door slam and sighs. She knows she could have handled the episode better—but how?

Few parental responsibilities are more important than teaching your children how to handle anger constructively. However, many parents feel ill-equipped in this area. When we observe our children handling anger inappropriately, we often panic and respond negatively ourselves, thus missing an opportunity to train our children. Having been such a panic-stricken parent, I write this chapter with great empathy for parents who are still struggling with this responsibility.

The reality is all children will experience anger. We don't have to teach children to experience anger. Our task is to teach them how to manage their anger. Because of the nature of the parent-child relationship, parents are the most influential persons in developing a child's pattern of anger management. This should encourage us, because it gives us an opportunity to give our children positive anger management skills. On the other hand, this can be a frightening reality, because if we fail in this area, our children will be disadvantaged as they move into adulthood.

As I talk to parents across the country, most are eager to learn how to help their children in this important area of development. Let me share with you the principles I have shared with many parents in the counseling room and in parenting workshops. They are simple to understand but not necessarily easy to do. Putting these principles into practice will require not only your best attention, but also the aid of the Holy Spirit. The good news is that when we are seeking to follow biblical principles, the Spirit's help is readily available.

LOVE COMES FIRST

Let me begin with what I believe to be foundational: *Focus on meeting your child's need for emotional love.* Why am I bringing up the subject of love when we are talking about anger? Because love is the foundation for healthy parent-child relationships. If the child does not feel loved by the parent, not only will the child experience greater anger, but all efforts on the part of the parent to teach the child are likely to be rejected. In *The 5 Love Languages of Children*, which I coauthored with psychiatrist Ross Campbell, I emphasize the importance of meeting the child's need for love. If the child's emotional love tank is not filled with parental love, the empty tank will itself become a source of anger. Something deep within the heart of each child is constantly saying, *Parents are supposed to love children.* If the child does not feel that love, there is a sense of being treated unfairly, and this gives rise to anger.

The five love languages—words of affirmation, quality time, gifts, acts of service, and physical touch—need to be spoken to children regularly. Every child has one primary love language that clearly communicates love to her. As parents, we can love our children most effectively by discovering their primary love language and speaking it even more frequently than the other four.

Such expressions of love must be unconditional. Without realizing it, many parents give love only when their children are in a pleasant mood or doing what the parents desire. These parents think that if they withhold expressions of love, their children will do what they desire. This almost never happens. When it does, the child is almost always rebelling inside.

Parents need not be pleased with the child's behavior in order to give the child a hug, a pat on the back, or an affirming arm on the shoulder. Parents can say, "You played a great game last night," even though the child's room may be a disaster area. A dad can take his son out to breakfast for quality time even when the son broke the rule and vase by bouncing the basketball in the den. A mother can give her daughter a new dress as a gift even though the daughter did not complete her homework.

"But won't this cause my children to be irresponsible?" many parents ask. The answer is, "Such love teaches responsibility." When the child senses that you love her and that love is not based on her behavior, she is far more likely to be responsive to your requests or your commands, and to do so without rebellion. When you love your children unconditionally and keep the love tank full, you have removed one of the prime sources of childhood and adolescent anger.[1]

WE DO NOT FILL OUR CHILDREN'S LOVE TANK AND THEN TAKE A VACATION.

The message our children need to hear and feel is, "I love you no matter what you do. I don't always like what you do or agree with what you do, but I will always love you." Children who feel the security of parental love are much more likely to make wise choices in life; and when they do make poor choices, they are far more likely to learn from their mistakes and to correct future behavior. Nothing is more fundamental in teaching a child to handle anger than giving the child unconditional love.

A child's need for love is continuous. Love is like food; it cannot be stored up—it needs to be expressed daily. We do not fill our children's love tank and then take a vacation. The love tank empties quickly, as does the stomach. The wise parent will discover the child's primary love language and give heavy doses daily, sprinkling in the other four regularly.

With this foundation laid, I believe there are three primary methods whereby we teach our children how to handle their anger positively.

"WE'VE ALWAYS SCREAMED AT EACH OTHER"

Scott and Dee are parents of Matt, age fourteen, and Missy, age eighteen. They are sitting in my office on a beautiful fall afternoon. The white clouds are floating through the blue Carolina sky, and the brilliant yellow leaves outside my window are dancing in the breeze. However, Scott and Dee are not looking at the clouds or the leaves; their eyes focus on my gray carpet. Scott begins their story.

"We feel like a failure with our son. Our daughter never caused us any problems, but we've always had struggles with our son. The main problem is his anger. This year has been the worst. Maybe it's because he is a teenager now."

"It's like he doesn't respect us," Dee adds. "He screams at me all the time; everything I do is wrong. And now he's started screaming at his father. We have got to have help."

With that information, I began a dialogue with the parents. "How do you typically respond to Matt's yelling and screaming?" I asked Scott.

"Well, usually I'm calm, and I try to listen to him and reason with him. But after a while, he becomes so illogical that I lose my cool and end up yelling at him. I know that's not right, but it's like

I don't know what else to do."

"And how do you respond?" I asked Dee.

"We've always screamed at each other," she said. "I don't think he should be allowed to talk to us that way. I scream at Matt, and when he leaves, I scream at Scott. I tell him that he shouldn't let Matt talk to us that way. I'm a wreck. Maybe I'm the one who needs help."

Dee's openness so early in our conversation surprised me. I could tell that she was desperate. She wasn't playing games. She sincerely wanted help.

"I'm glad you have come today. I believe the first step is always reaching out for help. I want to assure you that a lot of other couples have struggled with similar situations, and I believe that there are answers. But I want to begin by asking you a few questions that may seem to be unrelated, but I think will help us get a perspective on things. Okay?"

They agreed, and I began by asking Scott to recall his childhood and tell me how his parents handled anger in their relationship.

"My father was the angry one," he said. "I don't mean he was angry all the time. He was basically a good man, but once in a while he would lose his temper and yell at Mom or me," he said.

"And how did you and your mom respond to his yelling?"

"We both clammed up," he said. "When Dad started yelling, we knew there was no need to respond. I think Mom had learned that it would simply escalate matters. So if he got loud, she got silent, and that's basically what I did. Dad would sputter on for a while and then walk out of the room. And the next day, he acted like nothing had ever happened. It was never brought up again. Fortunately, this didn't happen too often, so most of my childhood was rather calm and good."

"What about your home, Dee? How did your parents handle anger?"

She smiled and said, "I grew up in an Italian home. We were always loud. Everybody screamed at everybody, but when it was over, it was over. Nobody carried a grudge; everybody had their say and it was finished."

"I want to make an observation," I said. "Scott, I think I remember you saying that typically in your response to Matt, you tend to be quiet, but after a while you lose your temper and yell back at him. Is that correct?" Scott nodded. "So you respond to Matt's yelling in the same way you and your mother responded to your father's yelling? Is that correct?"

"Yes, except that eventually I start yelling at Matt. I never did that with my father."

"And, Dee, if I heard you correctly, you said that you and Matt have always screamed at each other, which is pretty much like it was in your childhood home."

"Yes, except that Matt never stops. It's never over with Matt."

"The reason I ask these questions," I said, "is because most of us learn how to manage anger by observing our parents handle anger. And typically, we identify with the parent whose personality is most like ours. I haven't asked this, Scott, but I'm guessing that your personality is more like your mother than your father; is that correct?"

"Definitely," he said.

"So your most basic response to anger is to be silent. It's only after you are pushed to the limit that you explode and become like your father. Your parents had two very different ways of handling anger. Your mother withdrew in silence, and your father yelled and screamed. So you had two models. You identified most closely with your mother, but on occasion, you responded like your father.

"Dee, apparently in your house your mother and father yelled at each other when angry. That was their way of processing their anger. So as an adult, that is the method you typically follow. The difference in your marriage, of course, is that most of the time, Scott does not yell back; he becomes silent, and so you have your say while he sits in silence."

"Yes, and that makes me even madder," Dee said. "I wish he would yell back at me."

"And yet, if I understood you correctly, you don't want Matt to yell at you."

"Matt is different," she said. "He's our child; he's not my husband. Children shouldn't yell at parents."

"Did you yell at your parents?" I asked. Dee was silent for a moment and then said, "Yes, I guess I did."

Dee and Scott are illustrating the profound effect of the parental model. They learned certain responses from their parents—now they're modeling "anger management" to their son.

Many parents can identify with Dee and Scott. Often adults do not consciously think of their own anger management until they observe their children's response to anger. Many times, children mirror what they have learned from parents. Typically, as in the case of Matt, children respond to anger much the same way as the parent whose personality is most like their own. Since Matt was a child, when Dee was angry with his behavior, she had expressed her anger in loud tirades toward him. Matt now expresses his anger in a similar way.

Fortunately, adults can learn to change destructive patterns and establish new and healthier models of processing anger. Through several sessions, I worked with Dee and Scott, helping them understand the ideas we have shared in this book and watching them learn how to share their anger with each other in an open, loving, non-condemning manner. On occasion, Matt observed them talking and listening to each other as they discussed the issues that aroused their anger. He told me later, "I knew something strange was going on, but I didn't know what. I had never heard them talk that openly to each other without screaming."

Later on, Dee and Scott told Matt about what had happened: They had realized that their model of handling anger was not very positive and had decided to go for counseling; they were learning new ways to respond to their own anger. Matt seemed pleased, although he didn't say much at the time. However, they knew he was getting the message when one night as Dee was getting a bit tense, Matt said, "Mom, I think you need to get the three-by-five card and read it to Dad." Dee said, "I think you're right, Matt. Thanks."

They were really shocked one night about two months later when Matt walked into the room holding the three-by-five card and said, "I'm feeling angry right now, but don't worry—I'm not going to attack you. But I do need your help. Is this a good time to talk?" They both broke into laughter. Matt said, "No, guys, I'm really serious. I'm angry and I need to talk with you about it." They gave Matt their undivided attention—and let him talk.

TEACHING YOUR KIDS HOW TO BE ANGRY

Parents can also actively *guide* children through their own anger episodes. The parent recognizes that children cannot be expected to handle anger in a mature manner until they have been taught. Just as a child must be taught how to tie her shoes, write complete sentences, and ride a bicycle, so a child must be taught how to handle anger.

A child has only two ways to express anger: verbally and behaviorally. Each of these can be positive or negative. Behaviorally, a child may express anger by pushing, shoving, striking, throwing objects, pulling hair, or beating his own head against the wall. Obviously, these are negative behavioral responses to anger. On the other hand, leaving the room, counting to 100 aloud, or taking a walk outside are mature behavioral responses to anger that allow the child to cool down and process anger in a constructive manner.

On the verbal side, the child may yell and scream condemning statements or may use profanity or name-calling—all very destructive ways of verbalizing anger. On the other hand, the extremely mature child may acknowledge to the parent that she is angry and ask for an opportunity to discuss her complete concerns. That is a very positive way of verbally expressing anger. The task of the parent is to take the child where he is and help him move toward more constructive ways of processing anger.

Some parents have difficulty accepting a child's limits and imperfections in managing his anger. They want the child to be mature in his expressions of anger and are unwilling to allow the stages of immaturity. The parent who says, "Shut up. You're not going to talk to me that way. Don't ever raise your voice at me again. Do you understand?" is expecting perfection from the child. This is unrealistic. In fact, the parent is expecting of the child a level of maturity that the parent has not attained. As one young man said to me, "My parents yell and scream at me, telling me not to yell and scream at them."

If your child is screaming at you in anger, listen! Calmly ask questions and let the anger be expressed. The more questions you ask and the more intently you listen, the more likely his volume will decrease. Concentrate on the reason your child is angry, not on the way he is expressing it. Seek to understand what he thinks is unfair or wrong. You may not agree with his perception, but the purpose is to hear him out. If he thinks he was wronged, the anger will not go away until he feels that you have heard and understood his complaint. You are the parent, and you have the final word on what will be done, but your child needs to know that you think his feelings and ideas are important. Don't let the child's method of delivering his message keep you from getting the message.

After you have had a "listening session" with an angry child, later that night or the next day you might say, "I really appreciate your sharing with me your anger about that situation. We may not always agree, but I want you to know that I always want to understand how you feel. I'm not a perfect parent, and sometimes I don't make the best decision. But I really want to do what is best for you. I hope that we can both learn how to express our feelings more calmly, but however they are expressed, I always want to hear how you feel and think."

"MY PARENTS YELL AND SCREAM AT ME, TELLING ME NOT TO YELL AND SCREAM AT THEM."

If your pattern has been one of arguing with your child, perhaps you can break the pattern by saying, "I've been thinking about us, and I have realized that I am not a very good listener. Usually when you are feeling strongly about something, I also end up getting heated. I really want to be a better listener. In the future, I am going to try to ask more questions and really seek to understand your feelings, because I really do value your ideas and your feelings."

As parents become better listeners, their children feel more understood. The child still may not agree with your final decision, but your son will respect you because you have treated him as a person. If you listen and ask questions calmly, in time your daughter will learn to process her anger in a more conversational tone, and your shouting matches will be a thing of the past.

If your child is using some of the negative behavioral responses to anger, such as pushing, shoving, and throwing objects, focus on the anger first and the behavior second. You might say, "It's obvious that you are very angry. I would like to hear what's bothering you, but we can't talk while you are _____. Would you like for us to take a walk and talk about it?" What you are doing with such an approach is acknowledging the importance of the child's anger and expressing a desire to discuss the issues that concern him while acknowledging in a kind but firm way that you cannot talk until the destructive behavior ends.

Many times the parent's anger is stirred by the child's behavior, and the parent responds to the child in an equally destructive manner. Eventually, both feel bad about their behavior, but nothing is done to resolve the issue that originally stimulated the child's anger. Obviously, the parent and the child have a great deal to learn about anger management. I do not intend to convey that what I am suggesting is easy to do. Parents who have never learned to control their own anger may find it hard to imagine taking the approach I am suggesting. But consider this:

- The child by virtue of being a child is immature. She is still in process. Thus, her anger management is not yet mature.

- Parents are older and at least have had time to be more mature. If we have not developed a mature response to anger, let's at least admit that it is our problem and not our child's problem.

When we parents learn to handle our own anger in a healthier manner, we will then be in a position to guide our children in processing their anger. Children desperately need our parental guidance.

If parents do not hear the child's complaints and seek to understand why the child feels that way, the child's anger will be internalized and later show up in the child's behavior. Psychologists call this passive-aggressive behavior. The child is passive on the outside, but inside the anger is growing and will eventually express itself in aggressive behavior, such as low grades, drug experimentation, sexual activity, "forgetting" to do homework, or some other behavior that the child knows will upset the parent. If parents understood the extreme danger of passive-aggressive behavior, they would make every effort to listen to their children when they are angry, to hear the issues carefully, to seek to understand, and to find a resolution.

This does not mean that the parent must always do what the child is requesting. The child's anger is often distorted, that is, rooted in a perceived wrong rather than a definitive wrong. An explanation from the parent may bring resolution. The important thing is that the child feels that you are genuinely concerned and that your action reflects your genuine love for him.

Each anger experience gives the parent an opportunity to guide the child through the angry episode, deal with the issues, and find a resolution. Each time this is done, the child becomes a bit more mature in verbalizing her anger. There is less need for yelling and screaming because the parents are listening intently, and the child is assured that she is being heard. Such parental guidance is an extremely effective way of teaching children to handle anger responsibly.

"LET ME TELL YOU . . ."

Most parents want to start with giving instructions. "Let me tell you some things you need to know," they may begin. Without question, most parents know a great deal that their children need to learn, and instruction can be an effective method of communicating. Give instruction. But be sure the foundation of love has been set; such unconditional love provides part of a rich soil for growing a child's heart. If the heart of the child has not been cultivated by unconditional love, positive modeling, and loving guidance on the part of parents, the seed of instruction is not likely to grow. However, if these are in place and the child's heart has been cultivated, then instruction is an excellent method of teaching a child how to handle anger.

There are many methods and places for parents to give verbal instruction to children about matters related to anger. Depending on the age of the child, the following are effective ways of helping a child understand and process anger effectively.

For the young child, reading and discussing Bible stories that focus on anger provides an interesting format for instruction. Such stories as Cain and Abel, Joseph and his eleven brothers, Jonah and his anger toward God, and Jesus and His anger toward the money changers all provide key insights into understanding anger. Reading the wisdom found in the book of Proverbs provides excellent instruction in how to handle anger. Many of the proverbs relate specifically to anger management.

Memorizing key Scriptures is an excellent method of instruction for young children. Consider these verses, all from Proverbs: "Fools vent their anger, but the wise quietly hold it back." "An angry person starts fights; a hot-tempered person commits all kinds of sins." "Short-tempered people do foolish things." "People with understanding control their anger; a hot temper shows great foolishness" (29:11, 22; 14:17, 29). Printing these verses on cards and memorizing them with your children is planting seeds of wisdom in their minds and yours. Another great verse for your child to memorize is Ephesians 4:26–27 (NIV): " 'In your anger do not sin': Do not let the sun go down while you are still angry, and do not give the devil a foothold."

For older children, reading and discussing this book could be an excellent way of giving instruction on understanding and processing anger. Encouraging a child to write a research paper on the topic of anger is another way of instruction. Such research could involve not only reading books and perhaps searching the Internet, but also interviewing parents and grandparents for ideas on the source of anger and how to process anger constructively. This could be an exciting project for the teenager or older child.

Informal conversation is also an excellent way for a parent to instruct a child regarding managing his anger. For the older child, such an open conversation, allowing the child to ask questions and make comments, could be a springboard not only for discussing anger as a topic, but also for discussing how the two of you have processed anger in the past and what positive changes might be made. In such a family conversation, parents might share with a child their own struggles with anger both as children and as a married couple. Such openness on the part of parents creates an atmosphere for the child or teenager to express his or her own struggles or to ask questions.

Such conversations can easily be initiated by sharing with the child something you read recently. For example, "I was reading an article the other day on anger. It said that many parents are not aware of how many times they lose their temper with their children and say things that actually hurt the children; the parent never remembers what he said. I was wondering if that could possibly be true of me."

"Well, Mom, since you brought it up . . ."

When you make your anger the focus of the conversation rather than the child's anger, you make it easier for the child to be responsive and reveal his perceptions of you and the way you handle anger. Such conversations can be extremely instructive to a child and may also bring insight to the parent.

In teaching our child, it's important that we not come across as having the final answer to everything related to anger. The child knows better than that—she has been living with you for several years now. Far better to be honest that you realize that you are still in process, that you want to do better at managing your anger, and at the same time, you want to understand her concerns when she is angry. The child is usually willing to "cut the parents some slack" so long as the parent does not come across with a know-it-all attitude.

Children are usually willing to forgive us for failures in managing our own anger if we are willing to confess our failures. "Son,

I'm sorry that I lost my temper this afternoon. I didn't handle my anger very well, and the way I talked to you was not kind, and some of the things I said are not really the way I feel. I want you to know that I recognize that was wrong, and I have asked God to forgive me; and I want to ask you to forgive me." Such an honest confession will go a long way toward creating respect in the heart of the child. Children already know that what we did was wrong. If we do not confess, their respect for us is diminished. When we confess, their respect is restored. In responsibly handling our failures, we are teaching children not only what is right and wrong about anger; we are also teaching them how to confess their failures when they don't handle their own anger well.

A positive parental model, loving parental guidance, and instruction that does not condemn are in my opinion the most powerful approaches to teaching your children positive anger management.

HELPING YOUR KIDS HANDLE ANGER

1. Model healthy behavior. Your kids are watching how you handle your anger—and will emulate it. Parents who display positive changes toward their own anger will soon see their children improve how they manage their personal anger.

2. Guide your child through her anger episodes: Listen to her, take her feelings seriously, but help her deal with the issues and find a resolution. As a parent, you have the final word on what will be done, but your child needs to feel that you think her feelings and ideas are important.

3. Give instruction rooted in unconditional love, positive modeling, and loving guidance.

"As for me, I would speak directly to the Almighty. I want to argue my case with God himself."

JOB 13:3

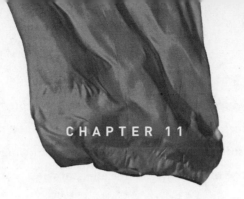

CHAPTER 11

WHEN YOU ARE ANGRY
AT GOD

Diane was past the weeping stage when she sat in my office, but she was white-hot with anger. Jennifer, her eldest child and only daughter, had been killed three months earlier by a drunken driver. The shock, the hurt, and the unmitigated pain had seemed almost unbearable to Diane. Now as she came out of shock into the world of painful reality, she was grieving over her tragic loss, and her loss was compounded by her anger.

Anger and grief are often companions in such situations. Diane was angry at the drunken driver who killed her daughter. She was angry with the judicial system that had allowed him on the road again after three DUI (driving under the influence) convictions, and she was angry with her estranged husband who had bought Jennifer "that little car." "She didn't stand a chance in that little car,"

Diane said. "It was a deathtrap."

As I continued to listen as Diane shared her thoughts and feelings, I felt deep empathy. I also knew that Diane's talking with me was a positive step in processing her grief and anger. Wanting to discover the focus of her anger and knowing that Diane was a deeply committed Christian, I asked, "What are your feelings toward God in all of this?"

"I hate to say this, but to be honest, I'm mad at God right now. I feel like He has deserted me. He could have spared Jennifer's life. She was so young and talented. Why would God allow this? I don't understand."

Christians often experience anger toward God in the face of tragedy. It is often true that the stronger one's Christian commitment, the more intense will be the person's anger toward God. As Diane said later, "I've tried to live for God and be faithful. Why would He let this happen to me?"

Diane was experiencing what Job must have experienced, for he too was a righteous man. (See Job 1:8; 2:3.) When God allowed Job to lose his wealth, his family, and his health, this righteous man felt intense anger toward God. Job said, "God has turned me over to the ungodly and thrown me into the clutches of the wicked." He lost his desire to live. "Only a few years will pass before I take the path of no return. My spirit is broken, my days are cut short, the grave awaits me. . . . My days have passed, my plans are shattered." (Job 16:11, 22; 17:1, 11 NIV). Job did not understand any better than Diane why God would allow such tragedy into his life, and he was clearly angry with God.

HOW GOD FEELS TOWARD OUR ANGER

When we look at Job and other biblical examples of people who were angry with God, it is clear that God did not condemn such anger. Rather, He entered into conversation with these people and helped them work through their anger. However, this does not mean that He always gave a full explanation of why bad things happened to good people. The book of Job is a long discourse between Job and his "friends" and between Job and God. His friends essentially accused Job of having done wrong and claimed the tragedy was God's judgment for his sin. Job insisted that this was not the case.

After listening sympathetically to Job's expressions of anger toward God, God's response was not one of condemnation. God reminded Job that His ways were not always understandable to men. He reminded Job that He is the all-powerful Creator and Sustainer of all that is, and that in the final analysis, He is a God of justice who can be trusted.[1] In the end, God expressed His own anger toward Job's friends for condemning him and urged them to repent of their wrongdoing and ask Job to pray for them. "My servant Job will pray for you, and I will accept his prayer on your behalf. I will not treat you as you deserve" (Job 42:8).

Job's ultimate response was to trust God even though he did not understand. Through this experience, Job's relationship with God deepened. In his own words, "I had only heard about you before, but now I have seen you with my own eyes."

> **THE CALL OF GOD IS THAT WE WILL TRUST HIM IN THE DARKNESS AS WE HAVE TRUSTED HIM IN THE LIGHT.**

The Scriptures then record that "the LORD blessed Job in the second half of his life even more than in the beginning" (Job 42:5, 12).

"WHY ISN'T GOD TAKING BETTER CARE
OF HIS CHILDREN?"

Clearly, God is sympathetic with His people as they pass through grief and anger. He is fully willing to hear our expressions of anger and to listen as we pour out our pain. It is not sinful to feel angry toward God. It is human. We have a concern for righteousness, and whenever we encounter what we perceive to be unjust situations, we experience anger. Knowing that God is all-powerful and could have averted these events, our anger is often toward God. "Why did God not do something?" is a question hurting Christians often ask. Theologically, we know that God does no wrong, but emotionally we experience anger.

When I ponder this question, two alternatives come to mind, for clearly God *can* do something. One, God could eliminate all sinful people and thus wipe out all the pain caused by their sinful acts. This, however, would eliminate the entire human race, because the Bible says, "Everyone has sinned" (Romans 3:23). The second possibility would be for God to step in and miraculously avert the consequences of all evil. God could stop all bombs from exploding, stall all cars of drunken drivers, eliminate all germs and viruses, still all storms, exterminate all fires as soon as the spark ignites, evaporate all bullets, strike mute all who begin to speak a hurtful word, or bring temporary blindness upon all stalkers and all who look with lustful thoughts. While this may sound inviting, it removes human freedom and makes a person a robot that must do only good deeds. Apparently God values freedom, and freedom requires the option to disobey as well as to obey. There can be no freedom without the possibility of evil, and evil always has negative consequences.

In addition to the injustices caused by evil, Christians often struggle with the apparent personal inequities they endure. "Why did my sweet son die from cancer when so many bad people continue to live?" "Why does it seem like I have so many problems when my sister sails through life?" *"Why isn't God taking better care of His children?"*

Such questions remind us that we have limited perspectives. While the Bible tells us something of God's perspective, it does not reveal all of His plans. Peter tells us that the trials that bring us grief may be used to refine our faith. Paul says that God can bring good out of everything, and that through every experience He is seeking to make us more like Christ. James indicates that our difficulties lead to our maturity. Jesus says that sometimes our problems are designed so that people can see the work of God in our lives. (See 1 Peter 1:5–7; Romans 8:28–29; James 1:2–4; John 9:1–3.)

While all of these positive purposes are true, they still do not answer all the questions that race through our minds in the face of personal pain and loss. The call of God is that we will trust Him in the darkness as we trusted Him in the light. He has not changed, even though our circumstances have been painfully altered.

HOW DO WE DEAL WITH OUR ANGER TOWARD GOD?

The problem with our anger toward God is not the anger itself but how we handle the anger. We could paraphrase Paul's words in Ephesians 4:26 by saying, "When you are angry with God, do not sin." Your anger with God is distorted anger. God has done you no wrong, but your feeling is still real anger. In fact, your anger is not a choice. Anger was your response to a situation that brought great pain to you and that you believed God could have averted. Thus, in your mind, God has treated you unfairly. Anger is the normal human response when we encounter what we perceive to be injustice. God made us with this capacity for anger. However, what we *do* with our anger is our responsibility. This is where we exercise the human freedom that God has given us.

The first step in responsibly handling our anger toward God is to *take the anger to God.* You need not be ashamed of your anger, for it is evidence of your concern for fairness. You can freely express your perception of things to God. You will not "hurt His feelings," nor will you stir up His anger. You are His child, and He wishes to share all of life with you. Your anger will not catch Him by surprise. He knows what you are experiencing and wants you to share your thoughts and feelings with Him.

"I HAVE HAD ENOUGH, LORD": ELIJAH'S STORY

Beyond Job, the Bible tells many stories of people who expressed anger toward God—such as the great prophet Elijah. In 1 Kings 18–19, we find that Elijah had confronted King Ahab with his sin and had challenged the prophets of Baal to a "showdown." Elijah had seen the demonstration of supernatural power when fire fell from heaven and consumed the sacrifice at Elijah's invocation. The people responded, "The LORD—he is God! Yes, the LORD—he is God!" (1 Kings 18:39). The prophets of Baal were then destroyed, and God—and Elijah—had won a great victory.

But Elijah's fortunes turned quickly. The next day, Queen Jezebel sent word to Elijah that within twenty-four hours, she would see that he was killed. Elijah was afraid and ran for his life. The word *anger* is not used in the biblical text, but we can read between the lines in Elijah's prayer: "'I have had enough, LORD,' he said. 'Take my life, for I am no better than my ancestors'" (1 Kings 19:4).

After this desperate prayer, Elijah fell asleep. In due time, he was awakened by an angel who simply said, "'Get up and eat.' He looked around and there beside his head was some bread baked on hot stones and a jar of water!" After eating, Elijah fell asleep again and was again awakened by the angel and instructed, "Get up and eat." Strengthened by the food, Elijah traveled forty days to "Mount Sinai, the mountain of God. There he came to a cave, where he spent the night" (see verses 5–9).

YOU CAN FREELY EXPRESS YOUR PERCEPTION OF THINGS TO GOD. YOU WILL NOT "HURT HIS FEELINGS."

With Elijah fully fed and rested, God initiated a conversation with Elijah about his emotional state. Elijah's response was, "I have zealously served the LORD God Almighty. But the people of Israel have broken their covenant with you, torn down your altars, and killed every one of your prophets. I am the only one left, and now they are trying to kill me, too." The Lord's response was not to argue with Elijah; rather, He asked Elijah to stand on the side of the mountain and observe. Elijah saw a powerful wind tear the mountains apart, an earthquake, and then a fire, but in none of these did Elijah see God. "And after the fire there was the sound of a gentle whisper. When Elijah heard it, he wrapped his face in his cloak and went out and stood at the entrance of the cave" (verses 10, 12–13).

Then God initiated another conversation with Elijah. Elijah repeated his prayer, expressing his disappointment that in spite of all he had done for God, he was now the object of a manhunt. God's response would seem strange to some. He commanded Elijah to anoint a new king over Aram (Hazael), a new king over

Israel (Jehu), and a prophet to succeed him (Elisha). God told Elijah that these leaders would take care of those who were opposing him. God also told Elijah that he was not the only one who worshiped God—that, in fact, there were seven thousand in Israel who stood true to God. Elijah accepted his new assignment from God, got up, and started on his journey.

We see from this story the value of talking to God about our anger. God is our compassionate Father and wants to hear our complaints. At the same time, He is also the sovereign God who does no wrong. He will either help us understand His perspective on our present situation as He did with Elijah; or He may, without explanation, simply ask us to trust Him as He did with His servant Job.

Elijah illustrates the second step in processing our anger with God: *Listen to God's message.* Having expressed our honest concerns to God, we are now in a position to listen to His "quiet whisper" to us. This sometimes comes through a trusted Christian friend or through a sermon by a faithful pastor. It may come through reading a Christian book written by a believer who has walked a path similar to ours. God's word may come through the words of an old hymn or a contemporary chorus, or it may come in your personal times of reading the Scriptures. Whenever God speaks, you will know it is His voice if the message you receive is consistent with Scripture. We listen to His voice, look for the good that may come out of this painful situation, and seek to grow in Christlikeness.

In the final analysis, we must accept what has happened in our lives, choosing to believe that though we do not understand it, God will use it to accomplish His good purposes. God's own Word, the Scriptures, and His very character as a wise and sovereign God, indicate He will. Listening does not always lead to understanding, but it does lead to accepting our situation without malice toward God.

This stage of acceptance may come quickly or it may take weeks, even months. But the believer who honestly shares his anger with God, eventually "will experience God's peace, which exceeds anything we can understand. His peace will guard your hearts and minds" (Philippians 4:7).

With this peace comes the full assurance that my life is in the hands of a loving God, that what has happened does not mean He has abandoned me. Rather He is touched by the feelings of pain that I experience and interprets even my anger as an expression of my love for Him. After all, why would I be angry if I did not believe that He loved me and would look out for my interests?

After the peace of acceptance settles upon us, there is a third stage. *We report for duty to get our next assignment from God.* As long as we are alive, God is not through with us. Though Elijah wanted to die, God had kings for him to anoint. You may be diseased, discouraged, disappointed, and in deep pain; but God has plans for you, and those plans are all good. "'For I know the plans I have for you,' says the LORD. 'They are plans for good and not for disaster, to give you a future and a hope'" (Jeremiah 29:11). As we get up and begin to do what God has gifted us to do, it does not mean that our pain has evaporated. It does mean that our anger is no longer a barrier between us and God.

Diane, whom we met at the beginning of this chapter, sat in my office over twenty years ago. Today, as she has done for many years, she is teaching a women's Bible study. Her classes are always crowded. "She has experienced what she teaches," one lady said. Diane does not seek to whitewash her pain and fully acknowledges that daily she thinks of her Jennifer and wonders what would have happened with her life if she had continued to live. Yet she also acknowledges that God has taught her much through the heartbreak.

Diane has many unanswered questions, but she is willing to wait for answers. In the meantime, she has chosen to believe that God is at work even in the most painful of life's experiences.

CAIN—OR ELIJAH?

Elijah was able to move on from his anger with God. On the other hand, Cain stands forever as the first example of how not to respond to anger. He lured his brother Abel to a secluded field and there murdered him. God held Cain accountable for his sinful behavior. Cain's life went on for many years, but it was marred by the sinful act he committed, which was motivated by distorted anger toward God.

Every person who feels anger toward God will follow the example of either Cain or Elijah. If we follow Cain, we will yield to our sinful impulses and in uncontrolled anger do things that will make our lives more difficult. If we follow Elijah, we will fully share our anger with God but also listen to the "quiet whisper" that comes from God. With much or little understanding, we will choose to trust God, knowing that He too is acquainted with pain.

For the Christian who learns to process his anger toward God constructively, the future holds hope in spite of the present pain. And for many believers, history will repeat the epithet of Job. "So the LORD blessed Job in the second half of his life even more than in the beginning" (Job 42:12). Like Diane and like Job, we will receive God's blessing, and He will use us in great ways.

QUICK TAKES
WHEN YOU'RE ANGRY AT GOD

1. Take the anger to God. Freely share your feelings. As our compassionate Father, God wants to hear our complaints. At the same time, as our Sovereign Lord, He will either help us understand His perspective on our situation, or He will ask us simply to trust Him.

2. Pay attention to where He may be speaking. God's "quiet whisper" to us may come through a trusted Christian friend, a pastor's sermon, a book, an event. Other times His purpose or simply His peace will come through music, prayer, or reading His Word. However it comes, you will know it is His "whisper" if the message you receive is consistent with Scripture.

3. Report for further duty. As long as we are alive, God still has "hope and a future" for us, a purpose whereby we can carry out His good plans.

Be at peace with yourself
and then you will be able to
bring peace to others.

THOMAS À KEMPIS

CHAPTER 12

"I'M ANGRY AT MYSELF"

The radio announces it is 65 degrees at 8 a.m., and Ron decides this is a perfect day to repair the steps leading to the deck behind his house. Within fifteen minutes, Ron is outside, hammer in hand. A minute later Ron hits his thumb with the hammer.

Waves of intense physical pain are quickly followed by waves of intense anger at himself. *How stupid! Why did I keep my fingers on that nail? I should have hired a carpenter to do this. I know I'm not good at this stuff.*

What is Ron experiencing on this summer Saturday? Anger directed at himself. He believes that the pain in his thumb, which is now running up his arm and making him dizzy, is because of his own careless behavior. His anger grows as he concludes that he made a wrong decision when he chose to repair the steps himself. *What an idiot. Now I might have to go to the ER. Day's ruined.*

Carmen has been dealing with a new job requiring a lot of

travel. Her friend Rose has texted and called several times and left messages suggesting they get together. Carmen keeps thinking she'll get around to responding to Rose's messages. The longer she puts it off, the guiltier she feels, especially because she knows Rose is between jobs and struggling. After a few weeks Rose stops calling. Carmen is angry at herself (*I'm such a bad friend*, she thinks). She would like to reconnect with Rose but isn't sure how.

From time to time, most people feel anger toward themselves. Usually it is because we perceive that we have done something wrong: We have acted carelessly, foolishly, or irresponsibly. In the heat of this anger, our thoughts are self-condemning. As with Carmen, anger is sometimes accompanied by guilt and shame.

As we have noted throughout this book, anger is an emotional and physical response of intense displeasure when we encounter someone or something that we perceive to be wrong, unfair, or unjust. When we experience anger toward ourselves, it is because we perceive that we are the ones guilty of the wrongdoing, the unkindness, the injustice, or, as in the case of Ron, the careless act.

"I KNOW I CAN DO BETTER THAN THAT"

Often, falling short of our own expectations can provoke self-focused anger. Jonathan was a young business executive, a hard worker, and a rising star in the company. But on Tuesday night, his wife, Kim, found him moping in self-condemnation. "I can't believe I left one of the most important elements out of my report. When my colleague mentioned it, it was so obvious. I can't believe I overlooked that. It makes me look so stupid, and to think the VP was there. He never comes to those meetings. I just can't believe it."

Jenna usually comes home from choir rehearsal in a positive, excited mood, but tonight Mac notices that she is quiet and with-drawn. "How did choir go?" he asked.

"It was awful," she said. "I don't know why I tried out for that solo. I should never have auditioned. I sounded terrible. I know I can do better than that. I don't know what happened. My voice just tightened up. I sounded like a screeching owl."

Jonathan and Jenna are angry at themselves because they did not live up to what they know they are capable of doing. They reason that not to do one's best is inexcusable. Therefore, they are angry with themselves for their poor performance.

Most of us sometimes act carelessly or foolishly. When these acts result in detrimental consequences, we tend to get angry with ourselves for being foolish or careless. Bruce was driving down a straight stretch of interstate highway in his newly leased car. He was focusing on his GPS when he ran into the back of a slow-moving pickup truck. He was furious with himself. *I can't believe I did that! I've always lectured Andy to never text or drive distracted. Keep your eyes on the road. I've told him that a hundred times, and now I do something stupid like this!*

Perhaps the area that makes us the angriest at ourselves is when we violate our own strongly held values. The Christian husband who is sexually unfaithful to his wife may try to blame her for his indiscretions but may later experience intense personal anger for allowing himself to fall into immorality.

Stacy, a committed Christian, lied about having completed a task at work. It wasn't a major project, but she had been putting it off, and when her boss asked if she had finished the job, she told her she had, not wanting to get into trouble and figuring she could finish the task and no one would be the wiser. But somehow her boss found out and called her on it. Driving home after work, Stacy brooded over the episode: *Why did I do that? I didn't even have to lie.*

Anger at ourselves over our own moral or ethical failure is often accompanied by feelings of guilt. Anger and guilt should lead to repentance and refreshing forgiveness, which we will discuss later. However, sometimes we wallow in our guilt and turn our anger inward.

"MY LIFE IS USELESS"
AND OTHER UNHEALTHY RESPONSES

Whatever the source of the anger we feel toward ourselves, we must learn to process it constructively. Explosion and implosion, which we looked at earlier, are negative forces we can turn on ourselves. We may explode through orally berating ourselves in private or with others: "I can't believe I can be so stupid. I don't ever do anything right. How did I do this? I am so ashamed of myself. I don't think I can ever face the world again. I wish I could just die." Such tirades may extend to physical acts of violence—pulling one's hair, scratching oneself, beating one's head against the wall or floor, cutting one's body with sharp instruments, even suicide attempts.

On the other hand, we "implode" when we attack ourselves mentally and silently. On the outside we may appear to be calm, but inside we are raging against ourselves. *I deserve to suffer; look what I did. I was so stupid. I don't know why anybody would believe in me again. I did what I knew was wrong. I don't deserve forgiveness.*

Sometimes the thoughts are highly condemning. *My life is useless. I don't deserve to be happy. I don't have any reason to go on living.* These are the emotional messages that play in the minds of those who internalize anger toward themselves. Such internal self-condemnation often has a detrimental effect upon the body and brings on physical problems usually associated with the digestive and neurological systems of the body.

Obviously, neither explosion nor implosion is a healthy response to self-focused anger—so how can we deal with this anger constructively?

FIVE GOOD WAYS TO BE ANGRY AT YOURSELF

Let me suggest a positive approach to processing anger toward oneself. The following five steps represent healthy responses to your anger.

First, *admit your anger*. Admit it to yourself, to a trusted friend or family member, to a counselor or pastor, but admit that you are experiencing anger toward yourself. "I am really feeling angry at myself" is the first statement of healing. Admit the other thoughts and feelings that accompany your anger. Perhaps: "I feel so disappointed in myself. I feel so stupid for letting this happen. I feel like I have let people down, including myself and God. I feel so irresponsible." Express as clearly as you can what you are thinking and feeling.

If you like, write the statements down. Say them aloud to yourself and say them in prayer to God. But admit and declare your anger.

Second, *examine your anger*. Anger toward oneself may either be definitive anger or distorted anger, as discussed in chapter 4. Definitive anger at myself means that my anger grows out of an actual wrong that I have committed. Distorted anger means that my anger has arisen from a perceived wrong rather than a real wrong. Both must be processed, but it is helpful to know the kind of anger that you are dealing with. There is a vast difference between the anger Ron felt when he hit his thumb with a hammer and the anger a husband who has been sexually unfaithful to his wife feels. The latter is an immoral act, and the anger is definitive. On the other hand, hitting one's thumb with a hammer is not immoral.

But it is careless, so Ron may choose in time to confess his carelessness to God, accept forgiveness, and seek to learn from the experience. He might pray, "Father, forgive me for being careless with the body You have given me. Thank You for Your love and Your forgiveness. Help me to learn from this painful experience. I love You and pray for the healing of my thumb." After such a prayer, Ron's anger subsides while his thumb continues to throb. He has handled his anger in a constructive way.

The husband who has been unfaithful to his wife has a much bigger issue to deal with. He has broken one of God's clearly stated moral laws. He is feeling angry with himself, and his anger is definitive, rising from a moral wrong. With his anger he may feel guilt, shame, and embarrassment. All of these are normal and expected feelings when one has violated moral principles. He feels guilty because he is guilty; he feels shame because he did a shameful thing; he is embarrassed because others know about his sinful act. His anger at himself is real and must be processed, which brings us to the third step.

> **WHEN ONE IS RIGHT WITH GOD, HIS DESIRE IS ALSO TO BE RIGHT WITH OTHER PEOPLE.**

Third, *confess wrongdoing to God and accept His forgiveness.* There is only one appropriate way to process anger toward oneself that arises from one's own sin. That way was prescribed by the apostle

John: "If we confess our sins to him, he is faithful and just to forgive us our sins and to cleanse us from all wickedness" (1 John 1:9). This is the clear message of all Scripture. God loves us and wants to have fellowship with us, but because He is holy, our sin breaks that fellowship, and He must treat us as disobedient children. This means that He will rebuke and discipline us. (See Hebrews 12:5–11.) But when we are willing to confess our sins, He is fully willing to forgive our sins. That is what the cross of Christ is all about. He took the punishment for our sins so that God could forgive us and still be just. Our part is to admit that we need His forgiveness. When we reach out for His forgiveness, He always responds in forgiving love and makes us pure again. Once again, we can enjoy His fellowship.

When our sin has been not only against ourselves and God but against another person, then we are to confess our wrongdoing to the person we sinned against and request his forgiveness. The apostle Paul practiced this in his own life. "I always try to maintain a clear conscience before God and all people" (Acts 24:16). We empty our conscience of guilt toward God by confessing to God, and we empty our conscience toward man by confessing to the person we sinned against. True repentance of sin is always accompanied by a desire to admit our wrongdoing and to make restitution to those against whom we have sinned. Confession is the first step in restitution.

Zacchaeus, the dishonest tax collector, demonstrated this principle when he encountered Jesus. Zacchaeus said, "'I will give half my wealth to the poor, Lord, and if I have cheated people on their taxes, I will give them back four times as much!" Jesus responded, "Salvation has come to this home today" (Luke 19:8–9).

Jesus did not forgive Zacchaeus because Zacchaeus offered to make restitution; his restitution was evidence that he acknowledged Jesus as Lord. When one is right with God, his desire is also to be right with other people. The husband who repents of an adulterous relationship and confesses to God will experience God's forgiveness. He can never experience his wife's forgiveness until he has acknowledged his wrong. If she chooses to forgive him, he then has the opportunity to work at rebuilding his wife's trust and bringing new life to the marriage.

Having experienced God's forgiveness and perhaps the forgiveness of the person we sinned against, we are now ready for step four:

Fourth, *choose to forgive yourself.* Forgiving oneself is much like forgiving someone who has sinned against you. Forgiving someone else means that you choose to no longer hold the sin against them. You will accept him back into your life as though he had not sinned, and you will seek to continue building your relationship with him. His or her sin is no longer a barrier in your relationship. If the wall is seen as a symbol of her sins against you, forgiveness tears down the wall. Forgiveness allows the two of you to communicate again, to listen to each other with a view to understanding. It opens up the potential of working together as a team.

As noted in chapter 8, forgiveness does not necessarily remove the hurt, the pain, or the memory of wrongdoing. But it does not allow these to hinder the relationship. With time, these will heal. Nor does forgiveness remove all of the results of sin. For example, trust is often destroyed when someone sins against us. Forgiveness does not automatically restore trust. Trust must be built by the repentant person being trustworthy in the future. If he remains trustworthy in the weeks and months after repentance and confession, trust will grow strong again.

These same principles are true in forgiving oneself. At its root, self-forgiveness is a choice. We feel pained at our wrongdoing. We wish we had never sinned. The reality is that we have. But we have also confessed our sin to God and received His forgiveness. If our sin was against another, we have confessed it and requested forgiveness, and we are seeking to rebuild that relationship. Now it is time to forgive ourselves. We must choose to do so. No positive purpose is served by berating ourselves explosively or implosively. All such behavior is destructive and thus a sinful response to our anger. This too needs to be confessed to God.

Choosing to forgive ourselves is best done in the context of prayer, letting God witness our self-forgiveness. The following prayer may help you express your thoughts and feelings to God.

Father, You know the wrong I committed. I have already confessed it to You, and I know that You have forgiven it. In fact, Your Word says that You no longer remember that against me. I thank You for Your forgiveness. You also know that over the past few weeks I have put myself down, beaten myself with destructive words, told myself that I am not worthy of living, that I deserve to be punished forever, that I wish I could die. I know that these self-destructive thoughts are not pleasing to You. Because You have given me life and because I have trusted in Jesus, I am Your child. I have no right to condemn myself after You have forgiven me. I confess these wrong attitudes to You, and I ask for Your forgiveness.

I thank You that You love me and that You freely forgive. Now understanding who I am—Your child—I forgive myself for the wrongs I have done. Even though the pain may follow me for a long time, and when I think of my failures I may weep, I will no longer allow my past failures to keep me from doing the positive things You have called me to do.

With Your help, I remove those failures from my life forever, and I commit myself to following You in the future.

Such a prayer, offered sincerely, can be the decisive step in forgiving oneself. As in forgiving others, this self-forgiveness does not remove all the pain or memories of your past failure, nor does it necessarily remove all the results of your failure. For example, if one's sin was lying or stealing, one may still have to face the results of those actions. Accepting God's forgiveness and forgiving oneself does not keep the thief out of jail. What forgiveness does is to release you from the bondage of your past failures and give you the freedom to make the most of the future. That brings us to step five.

Focus on positive actions. You are now in a position to change the course of your life. You can learn from your failures. Sometimes people make the mistake of trying never to think again about the failure. Their reasoning is, *Now that God has forgiven me and I've forgiven myself, I don't want to think about it anymore.* This, I believe, is a mistake. The fact is, we can learn much from our failures. The Scriptures indicate that God wants to work good out of everything that happens to us. (See Romans 8:28.) My part is to cooperate with Him. "Father, help me to learn the lessons I need to learn from my past failures" is a prayer that God welcomes.

What are the factors that led you to yield to temptation in the past? Those are things that need to be changed. For example, if you fell to the temptation of alcohol or drug abuse, it may be because you put yourself in a situation that fostered drinking or drug use. In the future, you must not allow this to happen. If your failure was sexual immorality, then you must remove yourself from the environment that would encourage you to repeat that failure. If your sin was fostered by not having a daily devotional time with God, then this needs to be built into your daily schedule. "What caused me to fail in the past?" and "What changes do I need to make to prevent this in the future?" are thoughtful questions that can lead to constructive growth.

In addition to learning from past failures, you are now in a position to take positive steps to make your future brighter. This may involve reading books, attending seminars, talking with friends, or counseling with a Christian counselor or pastor. These are the kinds of steps that give you new information and insights with which to direct your future. If your sin was against a family member or friend, this is the time to focus on positive action toward that person. I do not mean that you seek to manipulate the individual into forgiving you or thinking more positively of you. Manipulation is an effort to control another person. This is never constructive in human relationships. I am talking rather of acts of love that reach out to do something good to the other person without expecting anything in return.

"FATHER, HELP ME TO LEARN THE LESSONS I NEED TO LEARN FROM MY PAST FAILURES" IS A PRAYER THAT GOD WELCOMES.

Unconditional love is not payment for services rendered, nor is it a bribe to get what we want. It is a true effort to enhance someone else's life simply because we care about him or her. It is what God does for us every day.

THE POWER OF LOVE

When it comes to positive action, love is the greatest. The Scriptures indicate that if we choose to live a life of unconditional love for other people, God will give "us the Holy Spirit to fill our hearts with his love" (Romans 5:5). Loving is God's lifestyle. It is central in God's desire for us. "So now I am giving you a new commandment: Love each other. Just as I have loved you, you should love each other. Your love for one another will prove to the world that you are my disciples" (John 13:34–35).

Love is to be the distinguishing mark of the Christian. As you take positive action in loving the person you have wronged, you cannot force him to reciprocate your love, but you can be confident that love is the most influential weapon for good in the world. If your love is truly unconditional and is expressed in actions as well as words, you are doing the most powerful thing you can do for another person. However the individual responds, you will feel good about yourself because you are following the teachings of Jesus. You have been forgiven by God, perhaps by others, and you have forgiven yourself and are facing the future with hope.

QUICK TAKES

ARE YOU ANGRY AT YOURSELF?

1. Admit your anger. Write it down if necessary. Voice it to God in prayer.

2. Examine your anger. Is it justified—or are you loading yourself with needless guilt and shame?

3. If your anger toward yourself is valid, confess wrongdoing to God and accept His forgiveness.

4. Choose to forgive yourself rather than berating yourself. In prayer, let God witness your self-forgiveness.

5. Learn from your failures. Take positive steps toward ensuring that the wrongdoing will not recur.

A gentle answer turns away wrath,
but a harsh word stirs up anger.

PROVERBS 15:1 (NIV)

CHAPTER 13

CONFRONTING AN ANGRY PERSON

Sitting in my office one April afternoon counseling a young couple, I heard a loud rapping on my office door. "Pardon me," I said to the couple, as I stood and walked to the door. As I stepped outside, I saw a man who appeared to be in his early fifties. He wasted no time in stating his mission.

"I'll tell you right now, the church will pay for my muffler. Those speed bumps are too high," he said, pointing to the church's parking lot adjacent to my office. "They pulled the muffler right off my car, and I wasn't going fast. They should never have installed those speed bumps. If they tore my muffler off, they'll tear somebody else's muffler off. The church is responsible, and they are going to pay for it."

He said all of this without taking a breath and in his loudest staccato voice. His face was red. His eyes were glaring, and his nostrils were flared. I knew I was in the presence of an angry man.

I closed the door to my office. (Up until this time, my hand was still on the knob and the door still ajar. Perhaps subconsciously, I was planning my way of escape in case he got violent.) I said to him softly, "Now tell me again exactly what happened to your car." Again his angry words began to flow.

"I was driving through the parking lot, and when I went over that speed bump, it pulled my muffler right off the car. I don't know when they put those speed bumps in. They are too high, and somebody is going to pay for my muffler."

"Now tell me exactly which direction you were traveling and which speed bump you hit," I continued.

SLOWING DOWN

His voice lowered a bit and his pace slowed as he said, "I was coming from the activities building around toward Peace Haven Road. It's the speed bump at the end of this building. Why did they put a speed bump there? It's too close to the street."

"And did it pull your muffler completely off your car?" I asked.

"No, it's still hanging on at the back, but it's dragging on the street. I've got to find some wire to attach it so I can drive home. It's not right. The church should pay for my muffler."

Feeling that I had heard his story and understood the situation, I said to him, "I can see why you would be upset. I would be upset if that had happened to me. I didn't realize the speed bumps were that high, but if it pulled your muffler off, it will likely pull someone else's muffler off, and we need to have it fixed. I can assure you that the church will pay for having your muffler repaired. That's the least we can do. If you will send me the bill, I'll make sure that you get reimbursed. If I weren't counseling with a couple, I would go down and try to help you attach your muffler. But I think you will find one of our maintenance men on the first floor. Perhaps he could help you find some wire. I really appreciate your sharing this with me, because if you hadn't taken the time to come up here, I would not know that there is a problem with the speed bump. And obviously we need to have it fixed. I appreciate your taking the time and effort to come up and share that with me."

Now, more calmly, he said, "Well, I just felt like you'd like to know it. Did you say that you're counseling a couple?"

"Yes," I said.

"Oh, I'm so sorry I interrupted you," he said. "And I'm sorry I beat on your door. I should not have been so upset."

"I understand. It was a pretty loud rap," I said, smiling.

"I know. I'm ashamed of myself. I shouldn't have gotten so out of control."

Not wanting to add to his guilt, I said, "All of us sometimes get out of control. It's good when we realize it and are willing to admit it. I've been there. I know, but I genuinely appreciate your sharing the information with me about the speed bump. And we will have it corrected."

Backing away from me and moving toward the door of my outer office, he said, "Thank you, and again, I'm sorry I disturbed you." As he opened the door and walked into the hallway, I said, "It's okay. Thank you."

I had never seen the man before or since. But I have often used this experience as an example of how to respond to an angry person. Perhaps I use it because this is one time when I feel I did it right. (Incidentally, I never received the man's repair bill for the muffler. I can only assume he was too ashamed of his behavior to divulge his name and address.) The speed bumps had been installed two weeks before. As far as I know, his was the only muffler that was ever attacked, although we did have some complaints that the speed bumps were too high. The next week, we had them shaved.

THE BEST THING YOU CAN DO

From time to time most of us encounter angry people. Some are out of control. Others are trying hard not to be verbally or physi-cally abusive, but inside they are steaming over what they consider to be an injustice. It may be a neighbor who believes that you have treated him unfairly. It may be a fellow employee who perceives that what you have done is wrong. It may be a fellow student who accuses you of cheating or is angry with you because you will not cheat. It may be a mother-in-law or a brother-in-law, a father or a son, an uncle or a nephew, or it may be someone you have never seen before, such as the man with the wounded muffler. How are we to respond to these angry people?

Let me suggest seven steps. The first three are extremely impor-tant. *First, listen. Second, listen. Third, listen.* The best thing you can do for an angry person is to listen to his story. Having heard it, ask him to repeat it. Having heard it a second time, ask additional questions to clarify the situation. Listen at least three times before you give a response. That's why I call listening the first three steps in responding to angry people.

In the first round of listening, you become aware that you are in the presence of an angry person, and you get something of the person's story and the heart of why she is angry. In the second round of listening, she begins to see that you are taking her seriously, that you really want to understand what happened, and you are not condemning her anger. In the third round, she is scraping up the details and making sure you get the whole story; at this point, the individual usually begins to calm down, as she senses that you are trying to understand her. It takes at least three rounds of listening, sometimes four, for the angry person to get out all of his or her concerns.

If you respond to someone's anger before you have thoroughly heard his story, you will not defuse the anger. You will compound it. Inside the mind of the angry person is a deep sense that he has been wronged. He is expressing his anger to you either because you are involved or he thinks you have the power to help. When you listen to him, you are respecting his right to be angry. You are treating him as you wish someone would treat you if you were angry. This is what all of us want when we are angry. Why not give it to the angry people whom you encounter? Listening paves the pathway to understanding, which brings us to our fourth step.

Next, seek to understand the angry person's plight. Put yourself in her shoes and try to view the world through her eyes. Ask yourself, *Would I be angry in the same situation?*

It was not hard for me to identify with the angry man whose muffler lay beneath his car in the church parking lot. Had it been my car, I would likely have felt similar angry feelings. I may not have responded the way he responded, but it was not difficult to understand his anger.

It is true that sometimes the person's anger may be distorted. He may not have all the facts. He may be overlooking his own responsibility. My angry intruder may have been speeding through the parking lot. After all, that's why the speed bumps had been installed. They had been in place for two weeks, and his was the first muffler to be abducted. On the other hand, perhaps his muffler was hanging lower than the mufflers on other cars. These were details of which I had no knowledge and which were of little concern to him. It would have been useless for me to have raised those issues; they would simply have been attempts to defend the church and to point blame toward him. Both of these would likely have escalated the anger rather than helped to process it.

If you can listen long enough to get all the thoughts that are rumbling through the mind of the angry person, you will likely be able to understand why he is angry. Whether one's interpretation of the situation is correct is not the issue at this point. What you are trying to do is to understand what the person is seeing in the situation. Given his interpretation, can you see how he would feel angry? This is not the stage in which to argue with the person about his interpretation. What you are trying to do is to understand his anger so that you might help him process it.

WHEN YOU LISTEN TO AN ANGRY PERSON, YOU ARE RESPECTING HIS RIGHT TO BE ANGRY.

"I WOULD BE UPSET TOO"

Marina and Alicia worked in the same unit at a hospital. Marina heard by way of the grapevine that Alicia had told their supervisor, Barb, that Marina would be happy to work on New Year's Day because she hated football games and would like to have a reason to get out of the house. Marina had been chewing on this tidbit of information for the last two hours. As she did her work, she was thinking, *I really wouldn't mind working that day, but Alicia had no right to tell the supervisor that. She's simply looking out for her own interests and taking advantage of me.* Her anger was beginning to fester. Two hours later when the holiday work schedule was posted and Marina saw her own name on January 1, she exploded.

Later, on break, she went up to Alicia and said, "You had no right to tell Barb that I would be happy to work on a holiday. You had not asked me about that. Don't ever speak for me!"

Alicia, startled, had no idea what Marina was talking about but said, "Marina, let's go sit down. Now tell me exactly what you are talking about."

"You told the supervisor that I would be happy to work on January 1 because I hate football and would like an opportunity to get out of the house. Well, that's partly true, but you had no right to set me up to work on a holiday. That's wrong, and you know that's wrong. And that's why I'm upset."

The situation began to dawn on Alicia. "Are you saying that you think that I told her that you wanted to work on New Year's Day and that she should assign you that holiday rather than me?"

Marina nodded.

"Then I can see why you would be so angry," Alicia said. "It makes sense. If I thought that you had done the same thing to me, I would be upset too. I don't blame you for being angry. I would probably be angrier than you are if I thought you had done that to me. But let me tell you what really happened. Barb came to me and asked if I would like to work on January 1. I told her that I preferred not to, but I would be happy to if she couldn't get anyone else. I did say, 'You may want to check with Marina. I know she's said she doesn't want to stay home on New Year's Day. She might be interested in working.'

"I thought the supervisor would go to you and ask if you wanted to work. I was certainly not telling her to assign you to work without asking you. In fact, if you want, I can work on the first. It's probably my turn."

Alicia, after listening, expressed understanding of Marina's anger by putting herself in her coworker's shoes. This is the fifth step, *expressing understanding of the other person's anger*. Alicia told Marina that she, too, would be angry if the same thing happened to her. And by doing this, Alicia defused the adversarial dynamic of the conversation.

Once you understand the other person's plight (step four), let them know you understand. You stand beside her in her anger. You acknowledge you not only understand her anger but that you would be angry in a similar situation.

Having expressed understanding of the other person's anger, you are now ready for step six: *Share additional information* that may shed light on the subject. In the case of Alicia, this meant telling Marina exactly what happened in her conversation with Barb, the supervisor. It was the sharing of this information that allowed Marina the freedom to let her anger subside and to realize that Alicia had not wronged her. If anyone had wronged her, it was the supervisor by not checking with her before making the work assignment. But since Marina had actually wanted to work on the holiday, any anger she felt toward Barb was short-lived.

MANY OF US FIND IT VERY DIFFICULT TO ADMIT THAT WE HAVE DONE OR SAID SOMETHING WRONG.

Often the person we encounter has distorted anger; she does not have all of the facts or she is misinterpreting the facts. We do the person a great service when we share our perception of what happened. But if this is shared too early in the process, we will not be heard, and we will find ourselves in a heated argument with the angry person.

"Setting the person straight" immediately after she has unleashed her first statement of anger is a serious mistake. It will almost always spark conflict and seldom leads to a positive resolution. Friendships are often destroyed by such angry counterattacks.

It is important to share the facts as you see them but only after you have listened, understood, and expressed understanding for the other person's anger. Then your information will likely be received and processed in a positive way by the angry person. This leads to resolution of the issues and restoration of the friendship.

The final step in responding to the angry person is *confession and restitution*. If you realize that the angry person's anger is definitive; that is, you have genuinely wronged her—intentionally or unintentionally, what you did or said was unfair and hurt her deeply—then it is time for your confession and efforts to make right the wrong you have committed.

What would such a confession sound like? It would include accepting responsibility and asking for forgiveness. To try to defend one's own actions when you have, in fact, been wrong is an effort in futility and will again lead to argument and seldom to resolution. Many of us find it very difficult to admit that we have done or said something wrong. To admit failure diminishes our self-esteem, and thus we fight to be right even when we know we are wrong. Such behavior ultimately is to the detriment of one's self-esteem. When we know that what we've done is wrong and we defend ourselves rather than admitting our wrong, we may be able to convince others by our defense, but we do not convince ourselves. Our conscience begins to fill with guilt, and we feel bad about ourselves.

Defending our own wrongdoing is never a road to mental or relational health. On the other hand, confession and restitution almost always lead not only to emotional health but to strong, healthy relationships.

I believe that these seven steps are the most productive way to respond to an angry person. Let me urge you not to rush through steps one, two, and three. Listening, listening, and listening again is the foundation for gaining understanding so that in turn you can express understanding. In addition, recognize that steps one through five are crucial for creating an atmosphere where you can then share the facts as you see them and thus resolve the issue; or, if wrongdoing has been committed, lead to confession and restitution that can bring resolution. The other person's anger subsides because you have helped him thoroughly process his anger. And in so doing, you have maintained a positive relationship with the other person.

WRONG RESPONSE ONE:
TRYING TO CAP THE ANGER

A word of caution against two common approaches in trying to respond to an angry person. The first is trying to put a cap on the other person's anger. Parents are often guilty of this. "If you can't talk to me without yelling, then shut up and go to your room." Such a statement made by a parent to a child stops the flow of the child's emotions and bottles them within the child. Take two swallows from a Pepsi, screw the cap back on the plastic bottle, and shake it vigorously, and you will have a visual picture of what is happening inside the child whose parent made this statement. The child is in his room, the door is closed, the cap is on his anger, but inside the carbonated feelings are surging. When the cap does come off, you will have a child in rage. If the cap never comes off, you will have a child in depression or one who exhibits passive-aggressive behavior. That is, his anger will never be expressed directly but indirectly. By his behavior, he will do things "to get back" at the parent.

Seeking to put a cap on another person's anger is perhaps the worst way to respond to an angry person. The only positive response to such action is that the parent gets momentary calm, but that is a high price to pay for such temporary and shallow peace. We may not like the way the angry person is speaking to us, but the fact that he is sharing his anger is positive. The anger cannot be processed positively if it is held inside. It needs to be expressed, even if it is expressed with a loud voice.

In order to help the angry person, you must temporarily overlook the loudness of his voice, the glare of her eyes, and the intensity of the body language. You must look beyond all of this to the heart of the matter: What is the person angry about? What wrong does he perceive has been committed? It is dealing with this wrong that is the issue. Whether the wrong is definitive or distorted, it is real in the mind of the angry person. If we do not listen to the person's message, the anger will not be processed positively but will later show up in outrageous behavior, depression, or, tragically for some, suicide. Attempting to put a cap on another person's anger is an effort in futility.

WRONG RESPONSE TWO:
MIRRORING THE BEHAVIOR

A second negative way to respond to the angry person is to mirror his behavior. She is yelling at you, so you yell at her. He is calling you bad names, so you call him worse names. Such a response to an angry person obviously worsens the conflict. One angry person who is out of control is enough. We don't need two angry people out of control.

Thus, when you encounter an angry person, it is time to pray, *Oh, Father, please help me to be redemptive in this situation. Give me a listening ear. Let me get beyond the angry behavior so that I can understand why this person is angry and try to help him resolve it.* Such a prayer is in keeping with the admonition of the apostle James, who said, "Everyone should be quick to listen, slow to speak and slow to become angry, because human anger does not produce the righteousness that God desires" (James 1:19–20 NIV).

An angry person who is out of control does not need someone who will fight with him but someone who will wade through the smoke to get to the root of the angry person's behavior. A fire will burn out faster if you don't throw gasoline on it. When the angry person is spewing out words and you engage in argument with him, it is like throwing gasoline on the fire. An angry person can burn all night if you continue to throw gasoline. But when you listen as the anger burns, eventually the fuel of his anger will burn out. When he senses that he has been genuinely heard, he will become open for your help. But until he has been heard, his anger will continue to burn.

This principle also applies to our response to our children. We may be bigger and more powerful, but trying to dominate will not work. Paul admonished fathers, "Do not provoke your children to anger" (Ephesians 6:4). Responding angrily and harshly to a child who is trying to express her anger simply provokes more anger. And a key proverb advises, "A gentle answer turns away wrath, but a harsh word stirs up anger" (Proverbs 15:1 NIV). Whether the person is age seven or thirty-seven, harsh words thrown in the face of an angry person will simply arouse more anger. In contrast, an open heart that listens sympathetically and gives a gentle answer will cause anger to subside. This is the Christian model to which we aspire.

Angry people need someone who cares enough to listen long enough to understand the pain. They need someone who listens carefully enough to identify with the person's anger, wisely enough to express understanding, and courageously enough to respond with a gentle, truthful answer—an answer that seeks resolution of the issue that gave rise to the anger. That is our goal: to help the angry person discover a healthy response and a constructive solution.

RESPONDING TO AN ANGRY PERSON

1. Listen to the person. The best thing you can do is hear him out and begin to understand his story.

2. Listen to the person. Having heard his story, ask the angry person to repeat it. This shows that you really want to understand what happened and that you are not condemning his anger.

3. Listen to the person. Ask additional questions to clarify the situation. It can take three or four rounds of listening for the angry person to get out all of his or her concerns.

4. Try to understand his plight. Ask yourself if you would be angry in the same situation.

5. Express your understanding of the situation. Speak with compassion; affirm the person's feelings of anger.

6. Share any additional information that may shed light on the subject. At this point you may help the person realize that you have not wronged him.

7. Confess any wrongdoing and seek to make right the wrong you have committed. If the person's anger is valid and you have wronged him, this is the step to take.

AFTERWORD

A man or woman who learns to control anger responsibly has taken a giant step in Christian maturity. Many of the problems contemporary Christian families struggle with are rooted in misunderstood and mismanaged anger. Few tasks in the area of marriage and family life are more important than correcting this widespread anger mismanagement. Controlling anger will also benefit relationships with our neighbors and coworkers.

My sincere hope is that this book will serve as a catalyst in the Christian community to stimulate discussion, prayer, and eventually a clearer understanding of how to respond to the experience of anger. My desire is that you will not only read this book, but that through the self-assessment on page 211, you will learn more about yourself—and those you love. Additionally, the online discussion guide (www.5lovelanguages.com) with its reflections and applications will help you apply these insights in a group setting.

Finally, if you're married, I hope you will become a positive model for your spouse and children in how to respond to anger.

Let me suggest three ways you can apply this message in your life and the lives of others:

1. Share this book and its principles with your friends.
2. Suggest the book and the accompanying discussion guide as a study topic for your small group or adult class. Few topics are more pertinent to marriage and family—and all other human relationships—than the topic of anger.
3. Look for ways to help your non-Christian friends. Classes or conversations focused on proper anger management may be a bridge to a world that has lost its way and is increasingly driven by uncontrolled anger.

If Christians can learn to handle their own anger positively, perhaps God will give us the opportunity to share with our non-Christian friends. If we are not successful in dealing with our own anger, we may find ourselves "losing our cool" with our neighbors and thus confirming their suspicion that our Christianity is only skin-deep.

In reality, our anger is at the very heart of who we are. Tell me what you are angry about, and I will tell you what is important to you. For the mature Christian, anger will focus on true injustice, unfairness, inequity, and ungodliness—not on petty personal irritations. Such anger will motivate positive efforts to establish justice, fairness, equity, and godliness. Such anger will be tempered with mercy and humility, as the Christian also realizes that he—or she—is also capable of falling. To use the words of the ancient

Hebrew prophet, "He has shown you . . . what is good. And what does the LORD require of you? To act justly and to love mercy and to walk humbly with your God" (Micah 6:8 NIV).

Such a lofty lifestyle—practicing justice, mercy, and humility in our daily actions—requires first that we reconcile with God through Christ; that gives us the motivation to aspire. Second, it requires the daily empowering work of the Holy Spirit, which enables us to succeed.

Of all people, the Christian has the greatest potential for understanding and processing anger to the glory of God. That is the message and goal of this book.

NOTES

Chapter 1: Where Does Anger Come From?

1. Merriam-Webster's Collegiate Dictionary, 6th ed., s.v. "anger."

2. Mark P. Cosgrove, *Counseling for Anger* (Dallas: Word, 1988), 30.

Chapter 6: Explosions and Implosions

1. Mark P. Cosgrove, *Counseling for Anger* (Dallas: Word, 1988), 71, 95.

2. Ibid., 98.

Chapter 7: The Anger That Lasts for Years

1. See Romans 3:26.

2. Romans 12:19 KJV.

Chapter 10: Helping Children Handle Anger

1. For further information on how to meet your child's need for emotional love, see Gary Chapman and Ross Campbell, *The 5 Love Languages of Children* (Chicago: Northfield, 1997, 2012).

Chapter 11: When You Are Angry at God

1. See God's extended discourses in Job 38–41. Job finally responded in trust and repented of his pride (Job 42:1–6).

ACKNOWLEDGMENTS

Few people want to admit that they have a problem with anger. Most of us readily see the mismanagement of anger on the part of others, but seldom see it in ourselves. I want to acknowledge my debt to hundreds of individuals who in the privacy of my office have shared their tendency toward explosion or implosion of anger. They realized that their negative methods of responding to anger were having destructive effects on those whom they loved, and they sincerely wanted help. Many came with a deep sense of guilt and failure.

As noted in the dedication, their openness forced me to give attention to the whole matter of understanding and processing anger. Their willingness to be vulnerable has made this book possible. Without them, I would not have begun the search that led me to the discovery that anger has a positive dimension.

I am also deeply indebted to Tricia Kube, my administrative

assistant, who not only computerized the manuscript, but also daily answered numerous phone calls and did other administrative duties that allowed me time to write. Her assistance through the years has been of immeasurable worth to my ministry.

The Moody Publishers team have done their usual excellent job of encouraging, supporting, and guiding my efforts. Betsey Newenhuyse assisted me greatly with her editorial suggestions. Matt Turvey produced the self-assessment to enable readers to explore their own issues with anger. And Greg Thornton was my constant encourager.

Finally, I express my appreciation to my wife, Karolyn, who has stood with me through the pain and joys of life. On this project, as with others, she could not have been more supportive. Never complaining about my hours in the office, she always supported my efforts and prayed on my behalf. "Her children arise and call her blessed; her husband . . . praises her" (Proverbs 31:28).

PERSONAL ANGER ASSESSMENT

The following assessment is designed to help you understand how you manage your anger. Read each of the twelve hypothetical scenarios and check the box associated with the statement that most closely matches your response. It is possible that none of the three statements are a perfect match, but select the one that is closest.

I have serious arguments with my loved one, sometimes for no reason.	A	
I think most people would think I handle my anger well.	B	
When I am angry with someone, I am quickly and respectfully able to tell him or her why.	C	

I'm very good at being quick to talk to someone who offends me so we can work out the issue.	C	
I fly off the handle quickly.	A	
Sometimes it takes me longer than I'd like to get over being angry.	B	

I occasionally feel regret about how I express my anger.	B	
I simply let bygones be bygones.	C	
I find it very hard to forgive someone who has done me wrong.	A	

Little things don't bother me very much.	C	
I wish I had some better strategies or ideas for taking care of the anger I feel.	B	
I take frustration so badly that I can't put it out of my mind.	A	

I've been so angry at times I couldn't even remember some of the things I said or did.	A	
I consistently find appropriate outlets for my anger.	C	
I'm usually able to figure out what it is that makes me angry.	B	

I don't generally like being angry with others.	B	
I have said malicious things about others to get back at them when I am angry.	A	
I rarely if ever raise my voice in anger.	C	

I've had trouble on the job because of my temper.	A	
My temper has caused problems with loved ones, but we usually seem to work it all out.	B	
If I have anything to do with it, I don't let unresolved issues hang in the air with those I care about.	C	

I don't tend to get in many arguments.	C	
Some people are afraid of my bad temper.	A	
I've blurted things out in anger that I knew I needed to apologize for right away.	B	

Though it doesn't always happen, I usually recognize when I'm angry.	B	
I have control over how I express my anger in the vast majority of situations.	C	
I often break things when I'm angry.	A	

After getting angry, I'm still able to act lovingly toward those around me.	C
I sometimes feel like arguments with my loved ones just lead to more arguments and difficulties.	B
My anger tends to come out suddenly in strong bursts that often appear uncontrollable to others around me.	A

I just keep it to myself when I'm angry.	A
I am quick to forgive others who have offended me.	C
I'm usually able to resolve arguments with other people.	B

After an argument, I often find myself wishing I had thought of a better way to respond.	B
People tend to think I overreact when I'm angry.	A
I work hard to have all the facts before acting on my anger.	C

RECORDING AND INTERPRETING YOUR SCORE

Go back and count how many times you checked each of the individual letters. Then transfer those totals to the appropriate columns below. For example, if you checked A eight times, then write the number 8 in the blank above the A below.

_____   _____   _____

A   **B**   **C**

NEXT ADD UP YOUR TOTALS AS FOLLOWS:

Multiply the total number in C by two and add the total number in B.

$$\underline{\hspace{2cm}} \times 2 = \underline{\hspace{2cm}} + \underline{\hspace{2cm}} = \underline{\hspace{2cm}}$$

     C   **B**   **Total**

IF YOUR TOTAL SCORE IS:

19–24 you know how to handle anger

7–18 you are doing well but can improve

0–6 your anger is handling you

WHERE TO GO FROM HERE

Now that you understand your anger better here are some suggestions on how to handle it. Please match up your total score with one of the following three categories.

19–24 | YOU KNOW HOW TO HANDLE ANGER

Your responses indicate that you generally have a good handle on your anger. You are likely aware of what makes you angry, and tend to be intentional in processing your feelings of anger. You likely don't experience too many difficulties from anger-related issues in your personal or professional life. There's always room for improvement, however. Consider the following possibilities for future action:

Action Steps

1. Is there someone that you need to reconcile with? Perhaps you had an issue or conflict some time ago and you haven't taken the initiative or effort to repair your relationship. Assuming it's within your power and you can't foresee any significant and/or unintended negative consequences, prayerfully consider reconciling and rebuilding a relationship with this person. Dr. Chapman highlights some biblical strategies for reconciling in chapter 3 of this book.

2. Even though you're doing well in handling your anger, none of us are perfect. Maybe you have some unexamined anger that you haven't considered as it relates to your spouse, your kids, your family of origin, your self, or perhaps even God. Take some time to examine your inner life and ask God, as the psalmist did, to "search me, O God, and know my heart; test me, and know my anxious thoughts" (Psalm 139:23). Dr. Chapman has some great words of wisdom for you in chapters 9–12 to figure out new ways of handling these kinds of anger.

7–18 | YOU ARE DOING WELL, BUT CAN IMPROVE

Your results are indicative of someone who likely handles your anger well in many situations, but there are still times when your anger is handling you. Recognize the areas where you are doing well in handling your anger, but also be cautious that your anger is not getting out of hand in other ways.

Think about the situations where your anger comes out most often. Is it with loved ones? At work? What happens when you react angrily? Are you a shouter, or do you turn your anger inward?

What words do you tend to use? What feelings tend to come out when you're angry, and how do those feelings find expression, in good ways or bad? Consider the following possibilities for future action:

Action Steps

1. You would benefit from better understanding the distinction between good anger and bad anger. Definitive (or "good") anger, as Dr. Chapman describes it, is a normal response to genuine wrongdoing, injustice, or mistreatment. Distorted (or "bad") anger, on the other hand, is our response to others when we have incorrectly perceived a construed wrongdoing, injustice, or mistreatment. We don't have all the facts correct in distorted anger. Learn some other key differences between the two responses in chapter 4 of this book.

2. Some people look like they have it all together on the outside and rarely appear out of control due to anger, while underneath the façade they tend to simmer with unexamined anger. This "implosive" anger can be characterized by brooding or withdrawal, among other expressions. Dr. Chapman identifies key strategies to deal with implosive anger in chapter 6 of his book.

0-6 | YOUR ANGER IS HANDLING YOU

Your responses indicate that how you are currently handling your anger could use improvement. You likely have many difficulties stemming from how you express your anger and how you relate to others during times of conflict. Your angry responses in many situations are likely exaggerated and create additional problems for you. You also may not understand why you respond angrily in certain situations, or from where your anger is stemming. These difficulties likely demand further attention from you to either heal some broken relationships or to move ahead in a healthy way in other personal and/or professional situations. Consider the following possibilities for future action:

Action Steps

1. Your angry responses are likely driving people away quicker than you realize or want. It's important to take a serious look at your anger and how it is affecting your life. You will likely benefit from learning techniques that help you change your anger responses in the heat of the moment. While learning some of these techniques, however, you would also benefit from understanding what anger really is. In chapter 1 Dr. Chapman helps you define what anger is and where it comes from. Later, in chapter 3, you will learn a unique and manageable technique for managing your anger responses.

2. Proverbs 29:11 says "Fools vent their anger, but the wise quietly hold it back." Perhaps you've given vent to your anger for so long and in so many situations that it's hard to remember what it's like to keep it under control. Dealing with the long-term effects of anger can be difficult. You'd do well to make yourself very familiar with the specific anger management techniques Dr. Chapman highlights in this book. It may also be very beneficial for you to understand and identify the effects of long-term anger as it relates to your emotional well-being, something that's explained in greater detail in chapters 7 and 12.

An interactive version of the Personal Anger Assessment is also available online at 5lovelanguages.com/anger.

There you'll also find these helpful downloads:
- *Anger* Group Discussion Guide (PDF)
- *Taming Anger: A Guide for Moms Who Are Tired of Feeling Angry* (PDF)
- Printable *Personal Anger Assessment* (PDF)

STRENGTHEN YOUR RELATIONSHIPS
ONLINE

Discover your love language for free

Explore resources and tools

Locate LIVE events

Listen to podcasts

Share your story

Watch videos

Get free stuff

www.5lovelanguages.com

building
relationships

WITH DR. GARY CHAPMAN

Get practical help for your marriage or any of your relationships. Listen to **Building Relationships**, a popular weekly Moody Radio program hosted by Dr. Gary Chapman, the *New York Times* bestselling author of *The 5 Love Languages*.

www.buildingrelationshipsradio.org

MOODY Radio™

*From the Word **to Life***